Suffering Successfully

A Biblical Perspective

Fred Chay, Ph.D.

Suffering Successfully-A Biblical Perspective
© 2014 by Grace Line, Inc
Printed in the United States of America

All rights reserved. No part of this publication may be reproduced, stored in a retrieval system, or transmitted in any form or by any means-electronic, mechanical, photocopy, recording, or any other - except for brief quotations in printed reviews, without the prior written permission of the author.

Scripture quotations, unless otherwise noted are from the New American Standard Bible ©1960, 1962, 1963, 1968, 1971 by the Lockman Foundation.

Cover and book design by Grace Line, Inc.
Cover photo by Danny Burk
Back cover italicized text is from Dr. Dave Biebel

Library of Congress Cataloging-in-Publication Data

Chay, Fred
Suffering Successfully-A Biblical Perspective - A biblical analysis of suffering.

ISBN 978-0-9858958-4-6

1. Suffering. 2. Bible. 3. Christianity

To learn more about Grace Line Ministries visit
www.GraceLine.net
Requests for information should be addressed to GraceLineMinistry@cox.net

~Dedication~

The best way I learn truth is to see it wrapped around a person. Truth taught "incarnationally" impacts me.

For the past fifteen years I have enjoyed life together with, and seen the truth of the Bible incarnated through a group of godly people. We call ourselves, "Joint Heirs." Many of these wonderful people have taught me how to live and a few have shown me how to die.

Thank you all for showing me the way.

~Contents~

Introduction

Chapter 1   The Panoramic Picture

Chapter 2   The Perennial Problem

Chapter 3   Faith and the Silence of God

Chapter 4   The Purpose of Suffering

Chapter 5   The Framework is Everything

Chapter 6   The Salvation of the Soul

Chapter 7   Conclusion

Our heavenly Father understands our disappointment, suffering, pain, fear, and doubt. He is always there to encourage our hearts and help us understand that He's sufficient for all of our needs. When I accepted this as an absolute truth in my life, I found that my worrying stopped.
~Charles Stanley~

To endure the cross is not tragedy; it is the suffering which is the fruit of an exclusive allegiance to Jesus Christ.
~Dietrich Bonhoeffer~

Our efforts to disconnect ourselves from our own suffering end up disconnecting our suffering from God's suffering for us. The way out of our loss and hurt is in and through.
~Henri Nouwen~

When suffering comes, we yearn for some sign from God, forgetting we have just had one.
~Mignon McLaughlin~

You must submit to supreme suffering in order to discover the completion of joy.
~John Calvin~

We do not know what is coming, but we know <u>who</u> is coming. And he who possesses the last hour no longer needs to fear the next minute.
~Helmut Thielicke~

INTRODUCTION

Suffering is not only a problem to be solved it is a mystery to be endured, so said the late Flannery O'Connor. It is certain that suffering is a universal malady. And yet it often comes as a surprise to those who suffer that there is often a silver lining if one looks close enough and from a certain perspective.

Joseph came to understand this as he reflected on the treacherous and treasonous behavior of his brothers from a different perspective - *"You meant it for evil but God meant it for good."* (Genesis 50:20) It is as if "Melancholy is Hope's dark twin," but at times it is hard to see and harder to understand. It is easy to simply say, *"The secret things belong to the Lord."* (Deuteronomy 29:29) This is true. But our Lord did not intend to overwhelm us or leave us ignorant concerning the most universal of issues that drives us to our knees in prayer and humbles our spirit before Him. And so it is to the sacred scripture revealed from our heavenly Father we turn as we make it our quest on earth to understand; that we might glorify Him all the more. For He has not left us without truth to be understood and obeyed in the midst of a fallen and finite world in which we often experience suffering.

For 38 years I have been a pastor in the church as well as a seminary professor of Theology. As a pastor I serve as a shepherd and minister to people in times of tremendous turmoil and the tumultuous circumstances called "life." I have made many hospital visits and prayed for those with intractable pain and anguish. I have consoled the dying, and comforted the living. I have officiated at too many funerals to count, but every face is etched in my mind. I have counseled many parents regarding their children. I have talked people back from the edge of suicide and have sought to encourage those who feel their own faith slipping through their fingers as life's circumstances have tightened their grip. They find the words of Blaise Pascal fitting for life: *"I see too much to doubt and too little to be sure. I am of all men most to be pitied."*

I have faced the ever present questions vocalized in a thousand ways, "Why is this happening to me?" "Is God really there?" "I do not know what to do anymore." "I'm not sure I can go on."

My personal life and professional ministry have not been immune from times of trial and testing. I have personally experienced the hurts of life in the extreme. I have felt the sting of betrayal from family and friends. I have experienced personally the consequences of the pollution of politics found

Introduction

even in "the ministry world." I am personally acquainted with the perplexing questions and ever present problems that life prompts this side of heaven.

This is a book for those who grieve over a "useless death" or a "wasted life." It is for you who have received that call in the night that changed your life forever. It is for those who have experienced financial ruin, the loss of a child or a spouse. It is for you who wake up each day to a new 24 hour clock where each minute feels like an hour, hours are experienced as days, and each day is endured as an eternity because pain is your constant companion.

This is a book for those who have had the texture of their life torn and tormented by times of trial and testing and who may not be satisfied with the answers they have received to the questions crying out in their soul. This is not a book for those who have not been touched by the vexing vicissitudes of this life. It is a book for people who are all too aware of the reality of suffering and grief in this world and in their lives. However, it is also a book that intends to recalibrate our focus onto another world; for those who live best in this world focus more on the world of the future.

This book contains few stories and little autobiographical information. Its intention is to focus our attention on the God of the universe and see if He has anything to say to us who live under the shadow of suffering and the sting of death, and for those of us who are entering or living in "unmapped darkness."

There have been many good books written that contain excellent philosophies of suffering and have explained in a tremendous fashion that which is called "theodicy," reconciling the justice of God, the goodness of God, and the suffering of man. There have also been many wonderful books written at the very practical level brimming with heartfelt stories and testimonies of endurance and excellence of faith. Of course there is also a plethora of books that provide nothing more than platitudes and pabulum to people in pain. Their profit is only for the author.

The book in front of you assumes that you have read some of these good books and that you are still seeking answers because you still have questions and need wisdom that will allow you not only to endure and survive, but to succeed and to thrive. This is a book that is both theological in nature and pastoral in its impact; for only as we understand the mind of God through theology will we be able to live successfully in our fallen finite world which includes suffering.

If it sounds like I have been reading your mail, let me challenge you to read on and see if there might be some words of wisdom from our glorious God and His grace that might help those of us who are the people of God living in a fallen and finite world.

The Panoramic Picture

God moves in a mysterious way, his wonders to perform; he plants his footsteps in the sea, and rides upon the storm.
~William Cowper~

In order to understand the end it is necessary to understand the beginning. In order to make sense out of the present it is essential to understand the past as well as the future. The Lord God knows this and desires that we should be "in the know." And so, our heavenly Father has provided for us a panoramic picture of creation that stretches from eternity past to eternity future.

People who are reading this book on suffering are undoubtedly Christians who are looking for answers and have probably spent much time in the Bible to gain some divine insights. That being true, let me provide a very *brief* summation of the meta-narrative that encapsulates all of us who live out our lives experiencing and enduring times of suffering.

Paradise Created

The Bible begins with the beautiful creation story, which is not only a story but is factual history.[1] In it we see the greatness and goodness of God as He specifically, selectively, and supernaturally created the universe, the earth, and humanity. The Lord's perspective of His handiwork is that "it is very good." This is "no boast, just fact" as the saying goes, and only God is in a position to make such a claim. Here we have the idyllic situation of Adam and Eve in relationship with each other and in fellowship with God, given the role of ruling over the earth, loving each other freely and completely, and worshiping God in total unity. How long this arrangement lasted we are not sure, but we know that the next scene in our story carries consequences that are colossal, universal, and very personal.

Paradise Corrupted

The challenge came to Eve by the tempter, the serpent, the evil one. Misery loves company and so Eve then ensnared Adam to disobey the word of the Lord.

> *Now the serpent was more crafty than any beast of the field which the LORD God had made. And he said to the woman, "Indeed, has God said, 'You shall not eat from any tree of the garden'?" And the woman said to the serpent, "From the fruit of the*

---

[1] See the modern debate in *Four Views of the Historical Adam,* Zondervan 2013.

> *trees of the garden we may eat; but from the fruit of the tree which is in the middle of the garden, God has said, 'You shall not eat from it or touch it, or you will die.'" And the serpent said to the woman, "You surely will not die! For God knows that in the day you eat from it your eyes will be opened and you will be like God, knowing good and evil. When the woman saw that the tree was good for food, and that it was a delight to the eyes, and that the tree was desirable to make one wise, she took from its fruit and ate; and she gave also to her husband with her, and he ate. Then the eyes of both of them were opened, and they knew that they were naked; and they sewed fig leaves together and made themselves loin coverings. (Genesis 3:1-7)*

The challenge concerns both the word and will of God as Satan seeks to indict God's innate goodness. It is important to notice that "the devil is truly in the details" for Satan's accusation and temptation was based on a slight adjustment of the actual words of the Lord. Satan is described as crafty or shrewd. (Genesis 3:1) The initial challenge of Satan to Eve is to question the goodness of God by inferring the Lord is limiting and holding back something that Eve needs. He slyly says, *"Has God said that you shall not eat from any tree of the garden?"* Of course that is not what God said. *"The LORD God commanded the man, saying, "From any tree of the garden you may eat freely; but from the tree of the knowledge of good and evil you shall not eat, for in the day that you eat from it you will surely die."* (Genesis 2:16-17)

Notice God's liberality. There is not a trace of stinginess on God's part, only a concern for their safety. But the devil questioned the goodness of the Lord and distorted the scripture by failing to include the nature of the gift of God. The Lord said they may "eat freely," the devil removes the term "freely" trying to devalue the gift of God. Eve went a step further and twisted God's words by adding an additional comment, "we may not eat <u>or touch it.</u>"

God had not said this additional command. Finally, Satan utilizes the correct term but denies the truth of the statement made to Eve by the Lord. The Lord said if they ate of the forbidden fruit - "you shall <u>surely</u> die." Satan utilized the correct term but falsified the truth of the statement by saying, "you <u>surely shall **not** die.</u>" The Lord was direct with the truth, Eve distorted the truth, and Satan debased the intent of the truth of the word of the Lord.

Milton captures the situation clearly in *Paradise Lost*:
> *Of man's first disobedience, and the fruit,*
> *Of that forbidden tree, whose mortal taste*
> *Brought death into the world, and all our woe*
> ~Milton, Paradise Lost, Book 1, lines 1-3~

The consequences of sin led to separation from the Lord. Isaiah boldly declared a most universal truth:

> *But your iniquities have made a separation*
> *between you and your God, and your sins have*

> hidden His face from you so that He does not hear.
> (Isaiah 59:2)

The result of the archetypical sin is the transformation of the creation from paradise to pollution.

The apex of God's special creation has rejected His love and reduced the quality and quantity of their life that would now lead to death, spiritually and physically. This death will proceed through Adam's lineage and lead all to experience the ruin of sin. As the Apostle Paul declared:

> *Therefore, just as through one man sin entered into the world, and death through sin, and so death spread to all men, because all sinned.*
> (Romans 5:12)

As a result Solomon, the author of Ecclesiastes, writes: *This is an evil in all that is done under the sun, that there is one fate for all men. Furthermore, the hearts of the sons of men are full of evil, and insanity is in their hearts throughout their lives. Afterwards they go to the dead.* [2] *(Ecclesiastes 9:3)*

In our fallen and finite world it is true that all suffering is an actual result of what we call original sin. It is also true that because of original sin each of us has personal sin and this too leads to suffering. But it is not true that if a person suffers it is because they personally have sinned and are suffering the consequences of that sin. We can suffer the consequences of sin

---

[2] Not all scholars agree that King Solomon was the author of Ecclesiastes.

without being personally guilty of the specific sin. Many people suffer at the hands of another person's sin. So sin and suffering are connected, but they are not always individually, personally or directly connected. This is an important distinction because many people feel that if they are suffering it is because they must have done something wrong or they have sinned. This misappropriated guilt can also include levels of shame that are unfair, unnecessary, and unhelpful for spiritual growth.

The Person of God

It is important when trying to understand the plan and purpose of God and the problem with man that we also understand the person of God; for that will allow us to endure and excel in the midst of suffering. For the Lord does not simply wish for us to survive in this sin filled world, but also to thrive and succeed in our spiritual life development. And to do that we must understand the person of God and His mind.

The world has constructed many false portraits of God but the word of God will have none of it.[3] It is imperative that we have a biblical picture of God if we are to have any hope of understanding and thriving in the midst of suffering. Yes, I said thriving through suffering; for suffering is actually the handmaid and tool of the Lord meant to mature His people and lead them

---

[3] For an excellent look at some cultural constructions of God see *Your God is Too Small* by J.B. Philips. It is old but never more relevant for today's audience.

back to paradise to rule and reign.

But let's not get ahead of ourselves. First we need to know just who the God of the Bible purports to be. In theology this is called Theology Proper. In this field of study the person of God, both his names and attributes are considered. No other area of theology can lift the saints of God higher than to understand the God who is there.[4]

One would expect the Bible to be filled with a description of who God is since it is a book written by God and it is a book about God. If we do not have a clear portrait of who God is we will never have confidence to trust Him in the hard hours of our life or the dark night of the soul. C.S. Lewis reveals the danger of misunderstanding who God is as he warns: *"The real danger is of coming to believe such dreadful things about Him. The conclusion I dread is not, "so there is no God after all," but "so that is what God is really like. Deceive yourself no longer."*[5]

We dare not be deceived or distorted in our understanding of God. In fact the truth about the person of God must surely humble us. Listen to Philip Yancey as he contemplates this reality.

> *Accepting creatureliness may require that I, like Job, bow before a master plan that makes no apparent sense. In the face of doubt, I have learned*

---

[4] For an excellent book concerning the attributes of God see A.W. Tozer, *Knowledge of the Holy*.
[5] C.S. Lewis, *A Grief Observed*, p. 66

> *the simple response of considering the alternatives. If there is no creator, what then? I would have to view the world with all its suffering, as well as all its beauty, as a random product of a meaningless universe, the briefest flare of a match in cosmic darkness. Perhaps the very sense that something is wrong is itself the rumor of transcendence, and inbuilt longing for a healed planet on which God's will is done on earth as it is in heaven.* [6]

We so often spend so much time focusing on things that are finite and temporal that we miss out on that which is eternal and powerful enough to provide what we need in times of trouble. The Bible exhorts us not to simply know our self, but to know our God for that is true wisdom.

> *Thus says the LORD, 'Let not a wise man boast of his wisdom, and let not the mighty man boast of his might, let not a rich man boast of his riches; but let him who boasts boast of this, that he understands and knows Me, that I am the LORD who exercises loving-kindness, justice and righteousness on earth; for I delight in these things,' declares the LORD.* (Jeremiah 9:23-24)

And so what does the Bible tell me about this Creator who cares for me, this God who is there? Quite simply, *"Our God is an awesome God, He reigns from heaven above."*[7]

---

[6] Phillip Yancey, *Rumors of Another World* (Grand Rapids Zondervan, 2003) 50
[7] Rich Mullins, "Awesome God," <u>Winds of Heaven, Stuff of Earth</u>, Reunion Records, 1988

He is Sovereign in His Power

Remember the former things long past, For I am God, and there is no other; I am God, and there is no one like Me, Declaring the end from the beginning, And from ancient times things which have not been done, Saying, 'My purpose will be established, And I will accomplish all My good pleasure'; Calling a bird of prey from the east, The man of My purpose from a far country. Truly I have spoken; truly I will bring it to pass. I have planned it, surely I will do it. (Isaiah 46:9-11)

For I proclaim the name of the LORD; Ascribe greatness to our God! The Rock!
His work is perfect, For all His ways are just; A God of faithfulness and without injustice, Righteous and upright is He. (Deuteronomy 32:3-4)

He is Omnipotent in His Person

Now to the King eternal, immortal, invisible, the only God, be honor and glory forever and ever. Amen. (1Timothy 1:17)

He who is the blessed and only Sovereign, the King of kings and Lord of lords, who alone possesses immortality and dwells in unapproachable light, whom no man has seen or can see. To Him be honor and eternal dominion! Amen. (1Timothy 6:15-16)

Behold, I am the Lord, the God of all flesh; is anything too difficult for Me? (Jeremiah 32:27)

He is Eternal in His Being

Listen to Me, O Jacob, even Israel whom I called; I am He, I am the first, I am also the last. (Isaiah 48:12)

Before the mountains were born or You gave birth to the earth and the world, even from everlasting to everlasting, You are God. (Psalm 90:2)

He is with me and knows ME!

For the choir director - A Psalm of David. O LORD, You have searched me and known me. You know when I sit down and when I rise up; You understand my thought from afar. You scrutinize my path and my lying down, And are intimately acquainted with all my ways. Even before there is a word on my tongue, Behold, O LORD, You know it all. (Psalm 139:1-4)

My frame was not hidden from You, When I was made in secret, And skillfully wrought in the depths of the earth; Your eyes have seen my unformed substance; And in Your book were all written the days that were ordained for me, When as yet there was not one of them. (Psalm 139:15-16)

He Cares for ME as a Person

> *The LORD is my shepherd, I shall not want. He makes me lie down in green pastures; He leads me beside quiet waters. He restores my soul; He guides me in the paths of righteousness For His name's sake. Even though I walk through the valley of the shadow of death, I fear no evil, for You are with me; Your rod and Your staff, they comfort me.*
> (Psalm 23:1-4)
>
> *Let your character be free from the love of money, being content with what you have; for He Himself has said, "I WILL NEVER DESERT YOU, NOR WILL I EVER FORSAKE YOU," so that we confidently say, "THE LORD IS MY HELPER, I WILL NOT BE AFRAID. WHAT WILL MAN DO TO ME?" (Hebrews 13:5-6)*
>
> *I am with you always, even to the end of the age.*
> (Matthew 28:20-21)

The biblical description of our God shows that He is a mighty, magnificent, and majestic being that we have been given the privilege of calling "Father." He is in fact both powerful and personal in all His dealings with His creatures which is why the Apostle Paul declares, *"Blessed be the God and Father of our Lord Jesus Christ, the Father of mercies and God of all comfort."* (2 Corinthians 1:3)

The better we know God the easier it is to trust Him with our lives. As Twila Paris has said in her song; *"Trusting in You is so easy to do when I see You for who You really are."* When we see Him for who He really is, then we know that God is too kind to be cruel and too wise ever to make a mistake.

However, this life often feels like one big mistake, and suffering often manifests itself in our discomfort, "dis-ease," and depression, and can lead one to desire death.

If God actually is eternal, sovereign, perfect, powerful, and personal then what in the world is His plan? It is not that He owes me an explanation, but it is often easier to endure "what is happening" to you when you understand "why it is happening" to you.

Fortunately, our gracious God desires to let us in on His most perfect plan. It might sound counterintuitive and it may seem counterproductive, but God's ways are both good and perfect, and not only the right ways but also the best ways to accomplish His desires.

The Perfect and Prophetic Plan of God

How does one redeem and regain that which is ruined? How does the Lord maximize glory for Himself and the good for His creation? For anyone else the situation looks hopeless and would make us feel helpless. But then there is our glorious, gracious God who Jeremiah affirms with a majestic statement; *Ah Lord GOD! Behold, You have made the heavens and the earth by Your great power and by Your outstretched arm! Nothing is too difficult for You. (Jeremiah 32:17)*

And the Lord confirms with a rhetorical question by His prophet, "Behold, I am the LORD, the God of all flesh; is anything too difficult for Me?" (Jeremiah 32:27)

So what is His plan?

Paradise Regained

The Lord's creation has been compromised through the sin of Satan and the fall of man. All of creation groans and eagerly awaits the day when the Son of man and the many sons will rule and reign in righteousness. (Romans 8; Hebrews 2, and Revelation 20-22) The Old Testament describes the past process through the nation and people of Israel and the future person of the Messiah from Israel who will redeem and restore the people of God to God. (Isaiah 7, 9, 53)

The New Testament continues and completes the story of redemption. All the shadows of the Old Testament come into perfect clarity and shine as a brilliant light centered in the Lord Jesus Christ. As Charles Hodge declares; *"Fallen man, ignorant, guilty, polluted, and helpless, needs a savior who is a prophet to instruct us, a priest to atone and make intercession for us, and a king to rule over and protect us."*

And so, the ancient promise of a virgin bearing a son (Isaiah 7), is fulfilled in the Christmas story (Luke 1:31). An ancient promise of a sacrifice to take away our sin, seen as a suffering servant (Isaiah 53) is enacted on Calvary, by which the Apostle

Paul can declare, *"There is one mediator between God and Man, the man Jesus Christ."* All of this is historically testified by the wretched and vivid events of Good Friday on the cross, only to be miraculously verified by the resurrection from the dead on Easter Sunday. (Romans 1:5) The ascension of the Lord Jesus is the vindication and final testimony to His earthly work to redeem the world and make peace. (Romans 5:1)

    The final scene of the cosmic story of the Christ is seen in Revelation 20-22 where Jesus, the King, rules and reigns over all of creation. The millennial kingdom of 1,000 years (Revelation 20) is delivered to the Father with the result that God is all in all (1 Corinthians 15). The eternal kingdom is established. (Revelation 21-22) All suffering is silenced. All trouble is terminated. And all pain is a thing of the past. Man has been redeemed and reconciled to God, renewed through regeneration, and all of creation is restored to the Lord God. The themes of restoration and renewal spoken of in Genesis 1-2 echo forth in fulfillment in Revelation 22; from the restoration of the garden, to the tree of life for the nations, to the eternal light of God shining forth throughout all the creation, with the progeny and posterity of Adam and Eve, men and women of every nation serving the Lord in righteousness and truth, glorifying His name forever and ever.

Pilgrimage for Today

But we are living in-between the times of ruin and restoration. As Roger Lundin says, *"We are living in-between time that stretches between the certainty of sorrow and the hope of deliverance, between the full exposure of human cruelty and full disclosure of God's glory."* And in this day there is suffering, there is pain and trouble. Job was right. *"For man is born for trouble, as sparks fly upward."* (Job 5:7)

So where does that leave us? We perceive the panoramic picture. We recognize and understand the grand portrait of the person of God. But in the midst of the meta story I must live my story in the midst of the "sparks," the pain and the suffering. It is in this world marked by the human stain of sin that we are "seeking to articulate our lives through the grammar of history and fashion their meaning within the syntax of time."[8] And yet we often experience time as "the mausoleum of all hope and desire."[9]

Is this simply the unavoidable penalty for Adam's sin and the inevitable price one pays for being fallen and finite? Yes, that is true. But it is also true as Myles Munroe states, "Mans' soul search indicates that something he previously possessed is missing." Therefore, it is the realization that something is missing and the reality of our craving for communion with our

---

[8] Roger Lundin, *Believing Again (Eerdmans, 2009)* 22
[9] William Faulkner, *The Sound and The Fury,* 1929,76; cited in *Believing Again,* p.17

Creator that provides the proof that the better land of paradise in the past might be ours for the future. But by what means and by what manner do we travel? Come and see the way of Job, James, Jesus, and the way for us.

The Perennial Problem
He jests at scars that never felt a wound.
Shakespeare ~ Romeo and Juliet

If we are going to discuss suffering and understand the biblical perspective, let's make sure we define our terms. It is safe to assume that most of us have experienced various kinds of suffering. They may vary in description, but they all hurt in one way or another. Many are in the realm of physical pain. Sometimes it is chronic, sometimes severe, and unfortunately at times, it can be both. Intractable and excruciating pain that seems to be unbearable and unending can eviscerate courage and cause faith to evaporate.

Relational pain can be experienced with friends or family. It can include grief over the death of a loved one or the desertion of a spouse. Relational or emotional pain can be instigated by a sense of treason or a spirit of treachery. Alienation from a child or separation from a former spouse produces pain that seems to be unending. It is often accompanied by a sense of guilt or attended with feelings of shame.

   A third realm of pain has to do with the unique area of religious persecution. It is not infrequent that both physical and relational pains are a part of this aspect of suffering. Many if not most believers of the early church experienced some sort of suffering or persecution for their faith which often included family, finances, and physical suffering. It included both sociological and psychological aspects of life and often resulted in loss of life itself. Today most who are reading this book are probably not undergoing the trauma that was found in the early church. That does not mean there are not brothers and sisters in Christ who are not. We know they are and that there continue to be martyrs for the cause of Christ. But most of us do not undergo this type of persecution.

   However, the arenas of suffering and aspects of pain we do experience are all too real. No matter what type of suffering we are experiencing we all have the tendency to feel a sense of discouragement, dis-equilibrium, or depression by which we become disturbed and dispirited.

   What would it be like to have all three of these areas of suffering going on in your life at once? Most of us have had one or two of these aspects of suffering visit us in our life. Maybe we have had all three, but not all at the same time and not for a long time. But the scriptures, always seeking to be accurate and

The Perennial Problem

relevant to life, speak to us today and every day as they provide a portrait of a man who had just such an experience and the Lord expects us to learn from his experience. You guessed it! That man is Job.

In the wisdom of the Lord, the oldest book written in the Bible is the book of Job. Contained within the first 2 chapters of this book are principles that are essential and not optional if we desire to understand God's design for living in a fallen and finite world that includes suffering of every stripe and style.[10] Contained in this section are two cycles of tandem events involving a cast of Job, the Lord, and Satan.

Job was a man of extreme wealth and prominence in an ancient land. He came from the Land of Uz, south of Israel and east of Egypt, in about 4,000 BC. He was a good man who is described as fearing God, being blameless, upright, and one who turned away from evil. (Job 1:1) He was no low-life or bad seed that deserved all that came to him. His name actually means patriarch. (He had seven sons and three daughters.) He was in a sense a father figure of his day. This is a good man if ever there was one.

> *There was a man in the land of Uz, whose name was Job, and that man was blameless, upright,*

---

[10] I will not attempt to flesh out the wealth of literary detail and theological meaning that the book of Job provides. There are many excellent resources that treat these important issues.

> *fearing God, and turning away from evil. And seven sons and three daughters were born to him. His possessions also were 7,000 sheep, 3,000 camels, 500 yoke of oxen, 500 female donkeys, and very many servants; and that man was the greatest of all the men of the east. And his sons used to go and hold a feast in the house of each one on his day, and they would send and invite their three sisters to eat and drink with them. And it came about, when the days of feasting had completed their cycle, that Job would send and consecrate them, rising up early in the morning and offering burnt offerings according to the number of them all; for Job said, "Perhaps my sons have sinned and cursed God in their hearts." Thus Job did continually."* (Job 1:1-5)

Here then is a rich and righteous man who loved his family and loved the Lord. But we, the readers of the story, get a glimpse into the back story, the other side of reality, the spiritual aspects that are ever present and always a part of life even if unknown to Job or ourselves. It seems that in the wisdom of the Lord, He desires us to have a glimpse of the fuller picture and a metaphysical peek beyond the physical world of how life works. It will provide insight and answer some of the perennial questions that pose such difficult problems for us in the realm of suffering.

> *Now there was a day when the sons of God came to present themselves before the LORD, and Satan also came among them. And the LORD said to Satan, "From where do you come?" Then Satan answered*

> *the LORD and said, "From roaming about on the earth and walking around on it." And the LORD said to Satan, "Have you considered My servant Job? For there is no one like him on the earth, a blameless and upright man, fearing God and turning away from evil."*
> *Then Satan answered the LORD, "Does Job fear God for nothing? "Hast Thou not made a hedge about him and his house and all that he has, on every side? Thou hast blessed the work of his hands, and his possessions have increased in the land. "But put forth Thy hand now and touch all that he has; he will surely curse Thee to Thy face." Then the LORD said to Satan, "Behold, all that he has is in your power, only do not put forth your hand on him." So, Satan departed from the presence of the LORD. (Job 1:6-12)*

Please notice some essential truths. The first observation is that the Lord is sovereign over every place and every person. Job is God's servant and God is Satan's master. (Satan has come to God's gathering.)

The second observation in light of the first is that Satan serves the Lord and is instructed by the Lord to accomplish His will. The third observation is that Satan always seeks to counter God's word and harm God's people. (After all, "Satan" means "Adversary.") And so a challenge is issued by Satan and accepted by the Lord and Job is in the middle. Now if you ever think you have had "one of those days," take a look at Job's bad day:

Now it happened on the day when his sons and his daughters were eating and drinking wine in their oldest brother's house that a messenger came to Job and said, "The oxen were plowing and the donkeys feeding beside them, and the Sabeans attacked and took them. They also slew the servants with the edge of the sword, and I alone have escaped to tell you." While he was still speaking, another also came and said, "The fire of God fell from heaven and burned up the sheep and the servants and consumed them, and I alone have escaped to tell you." While he was still speaking, another also came and said, "The Chaldeans formed three bands and made a raid on the camels and took them and slew the servants with the edge of the sword; and I alone have escaped to tell you." While he was still speaking, another also came and said, "Your sons and your daughters were eating and drinking wine in their oldest brother's house, and behold, a great wind came from across the wilderness and struck the four corners of the house, and it fell on the young people and they died; and I alone have escaped to tell you." Then Job arose and tore his robe and shaved his head, and he fell to the ground and worshiped. And he said, "Naked I came from my mother's womb, And naked I shall return there. The LORD gave and the LORD has taken away. Blessed be the name of the LORD." Through all this Job did not sin nor did he blame God. (Job 1:13-22)

The description of the devastation is written in a rhythm and cadence that seems to be never ending. The pace of the destruction is unending. Report upon report declares and describes the damage done to this man. Notice the type of suffering that has come upon Job. His financial ruin is total. This will create sociological estrangement, for most consider the loss of wealth a punishment from God. But the financial devastation is only outdone by his family's demise and the death of his ten children. But mark it well, at the end of the endless series of bad news Job issues a statement of ultimate reality as he declares: "Blessed be the name of the Lord." The divine evaluation upon such a response was: "Through all this Job did not sin nor did he blame God."

But this is not the end of the story. The second cycle of events takes us back to the presence of the Lord with Satan returning in order to inflict more damage.

> *Again, there was a day when the sons of God came to present themselves before the LORD, and Satan also came among them to present himself before the LORD. And the LORD said to Satan, "Where have you come from?" Then Satan answered the LORD and said, "From roaming about on the earth, and walking around on it." And the LORD said to Satan, "Have you considered My servant Job? For there is no one like him on the earth, a blameless and upright man fearing God and turning away from evil. And he still holds fast his integrity, although you incited Me against him, to ruin him without cause." (Job 2:1-3)*

Same song second verse; but notice a profound theological statement. The Lord takes responsibility for the evil that was enacted upon Job. The Lord says, "And he still holds fast his integrity, although you <u>incited Me against him</u>, to ruin him <u>without cause</u>." Job did not deserve any punishment and yet God takes responsibility for causing it. Granted, we are not saying God does evil (James 1, Habakkuk 1) but that He utilized secondary causation, Satan. The Lord declares He is the final cause, the responsible party for the events that befell Job. In the full view of reality, both physical and metaphysical, there are no accidents, only divine incidents.

The Adversary wastes no time in issuing a challenge to the Lord's assessment of Job by issuing another evaluation of Job's integrity. "Let me harm his body and he will curse you to your face." Satan has no shame as he doubles down on the outcome of the contest. The rest of the story is proverbial.

> *And Satan answered the LORD and said, "Skin for skin! Yes, all that a man has he will give for his life. "However, put forth Thy hand, now, and touch his bone and his flesh; he will curse Thee to Thy face." So the LORD said to Satan, "Behold, he is in your power, only spare his life.*
> *Then Satan went out from the presence of the LORD, and smote Job with sore boils from the sole of his foot to the crown of his head. And he took a potsherd to scrape himself while he was sitting among the ashes. Then his wife said to him, "Do you still hold fast your integrity? Curse God and die!"*

But he said to her, "You speak as one of the foolish women speaks. Shall we indeed accept good from God and not accept adversity?" In all this, Job did not sin with his lips. (Job 2:4-10)

Again, the rules of the game are determined by the sovereign Lord. Again, Satan takes it to the limit by inflicting horrific personal, physical suffering that would end up with Job's public ridicule. But again Job's response is textbook perfect. "In all this, Job did not sin with his lips."

It is interesting to note that the Lord comments on the fact that Job held fast his "integrity" (2:3) and in the end it is Job's wife who seeks to get him to let go of his "integrity." (Isn't it interesting that all of the livestock and children were taken, but not the wife? But then again most people would have given Job this advice if only to put him out of his misery.)

But notice Job's perspective. Good days and bad days; days of joy and days of adversity are from the Lord. They must be since He is the sovereign who orchestrates, allows or causes the events of life. Sometimes these are with and through Satan or other means, like Paul's thorn in the flesh was a messenger from Satan sent by God (2 Corinthians 12:7-9) but at the end of the day there are no accidents, only divine incidents!

Job is presented as the archetypical person who endures sociological, emotional, relational, familial, financial, and physical suffering. Satan is presented as the adversary who seeks to challenge God by harming His creation; inflicting an assault with a full assortment and an alarming array of suffering of every kind. The Lord is seen as the sovereign one who restricts evil and directs events in order to accomplish His will in and through His people. Job is the quintessential presentation of the human dilemma living in a fallen and finite world. The story of Job presents both a portrait and a paradigm by which mankind is to observe and learn of the greatness and goodness of God, the malevolent evil of Satan, and the potential response of man in the midst of times of temptation, trial, and testing. Job represents suffering personified with all its difficulties in every area of life. Job issues a challenge to any person who is suffering; inquiring of those on the brink of a breaking faith, how will you think and how will you act in relation to the Lord?

Not much has changed in four thousand years. God has not changed and neither has Satan. The only player that has changed in the story is Job. Job is me. Job is you.

We are not given a backstage look at the discussion between God and Satan regarding us. It is fruitless and perhaps dangerous to speculate on how that works. It is enough to know that life on planet earth until the new earth comes is filled with difficulty and teeming with trouble. Job proverbially states: *For man is born for trouble, as sparks fly upward. But as for me, I would seek God, and I would place my cause before God; who does great and unsearchable things, wonders without number.* (Job 5:7-9) If we could understand that both sides of the equation are true we would be better off. Difficulties are our destiny in a fallen and finite world. We cannot wish or will them away. They are part of the way of life. But the Lord is with us all the way.

I do not know you and you do not know me, but I know this: we all have dealt with and will continue to deal with suffering this side of heaven. It may be within our family or about our family. It might be physical or relational. It may include issues with our finances or our friends. But make no mistake, it will not feel good and we will wish that it would just stop. But never forget that God is in control. He has no rivals. There is nothing He is unaware of or anything that controls or constrains Him. *"I am the Lord God of all flesh. Is there anything too difficult for me?"* (Jeremiah 32:17-18, 27) These are powerful statements about His person and if they seem too distant, disengaged, or disconnected from you, then always remember; His power is also personal and God is too kind to be cruel and too wise to ever make a mistake. Job knew this in the midst of all of his anguish. I tend to forget it in the midst of mine. How about you?

Suffering Successfully

The Purpose of Suffering

Any idiot can face a crisis - it's day to day living that wears you out. ~Anton Chekhov~

It is said a person can endure most anything if they know the purpose behind it. Unfortunately we do not always know "what" is happening, let alone "why" it is happening to us. The fact is that often in our lives we experience events that seem totally unnecessary and unwanted. It seems as Flannery O'Connor said, "Suffering is not only a problem to be solved it is a mystery to be endured."

Make no mistake, if you live long enough you will face difficulty in your life. There are some who deny that suffering is to be a part of life. This is the teaching of Buddhism, and unfortunately some Christians teach that God does not want His children to suffer but to only experience health and wealth. That has not been my experience nor has it been for the history of the church. The fact is, life hurts and it can take a toll on people. It is true as Paul said in Romans 8 that *"...all things work together for good to those who love God..."* But I ask you as I ask myself, is that it? Are we left simply to go forward, nobly encountering and blindly enduring whatever comes our way? Or, are we permitted to deduce and become able to know some aspect that can strengthen our resolve?

The earliest book written in the New Testament is one that from start to finish details for us how to endure trials, testing, and temptation in the midst of the Christian life. In fact, the Book of James not only tells us "how to suffer and survive" but also "why" it is our fate and fortune, our destiny and delight to endure suffering and succeed. Through it all we learn the secret of how we can turn a life that seems to be a lemon into lemonade. James is writing to a group of Jewish Christians who have been dispersed from their homeland and are living in a foreign place enduring distress that is creating a sense of personal dis-equilibrium. Undoubtedly there are both physical and spiritual difficulties, as well as the attending family issues that accompany life. These people were in a real pressure cooker and needed to know how to survive. James explains how they can not only survive but how they can actually succeed. As we consider the words of the Book of James we must not forget that what we are reading is the very Word of God. This book is inspired and comes from God Himself, so it demands our attention and our affection. The Lord is mindful of our situations and as such has provided for us the means to grow in godliness. We must be ready to receive His Word.

The key to understanding the purpose for times of trial and testing in our lives is to realize that: <u>Testing Produces True Christian Character</u>. James provides two potential products in the Christian life that can only come from times of trial and testing. The first is by producing needed endurance:

> *Consider it all joy, my brethren, when you encounter various trials, knowing that the testing of your faith produces endurance. And let endurance have its perfect result, that you may be perfect and complete, lacking in nothing. (James 1:2)*

Notice James begins with the request. Actually, James expresses himself with an imperative; *"consider or count it all joy."* This is not an option, it is a command. Notice also that although the command can be disobeyed, the fact that trials will come into your life is not optional, it is inevitable. Mark it well, it is "<u>when</u> you encounter various trials." It is *"when they come,"* not *"if they come."* We know they come. It does not matter who you are, trials will come into your life. It is as they say, *you can run but you cannot hide.* Trials will find you out.

It is true that we do not all deal with the same issues in life. They come in a variety of colors. In fact, James uses the Greek term for trials that sounds like the English word for polka-dot and is translated as *"various or multicolored times of testing."* If ever there was a word for the ages, this is it: "testing." This term can be understood in a variety of ways both in Greek and English. Actually, the term is neutral and the context must decide if it is to be understood and interpreted as a trial, a test or temptation. In fact, the same term is used in Matthew 4:1 as "the Holy Spirit led Jesus into the desert to *test* Him." The word could be translated "tempt" but the context seems to demand a more positive connotation like "test." In the Book of James, the term is used frequently and context must determine its meaning. James is commanding Christians to consider that when testing of all stripes, sizes, and shapes comes into our life, we are to see it as a blessing. For some, times of testing involve physical suffering, for others it is financial --- *too much month at the end of the money*. Others struggle with relational issues that have harmed or destroyed families.

Now if I am commanded to be joyful when life seems to be anything but; I need a reason! The reason for the request is that it is only testing that can produce endurance. James says you need to know this. You need a frame of mind in the midst of life that realizes and knows troubles will come, they will visit your home, and you need to know what to do and why to do it. The reason we are to view the vexing vicissitudes of life in a positive light is that they provide a unique opportunity. It is the opportunity to develop within myself the ability to stay under the pressure. The only way to endure is to be under something, to be pressed or be squeezed by the circumstances and situations in our life. This is true in athletics, academics, and all areas of life.

The Purpose of Suffering

The only way to know and show you are maturing is to go through a time of testing. You must enter a time of examination. Since I am a seminary professor, I know there are many forms of testing that can give students the opportunity to manifest what they have learned. But regardless of the type of test, there needs to be a time that is uncomfortable so their understanding and performance can be evaluated. Testing is how I know what they know. Good teachers not only tell students what is to be expected, but they also let them know that what they know will be inspected.

I am a pragmatist. I not only need a reason for the request, I also need to know what the result might be. The Lord knows there are people like me, and maybe you, who need some motivation for the mandate, especially when it involves suffering. So, the Lord through James graciously provides us with a motive. The potential result of times of testing is that we might grow up. *"And let endurance have its perfect result, so that you may be perfect and complete, lacking in nothing."*

Notice there are three facets to the perfect result of endurance. First, that you might become "perfect." The perfect result is that you might become perfect. The term means "mature as an adult person" or fully developed and morally wise. Wisdom comes through experience. In Hebrews 5:7-9 Jesus Himself learned obedience through the things He suffered and as a result He became mature, fully developed, as He displayed His ability to obey God and demonstrate moral wisdom. But He had to go through some difficult situations, for wisdom can only be displayed in the midst of difficulty.

The second result is that we might become "complete." The term means to be whole, sound, and intact. It can have a moral quality as well. The idea of "blameless" might fit. These two aspects are stated in a positive manner. It is the idea of being mature, complete or fully developed. James summarizes and switches to a negative phrase, but it is not a normal negative. It is a double negative; "lacking nothing" or "not lacking" and actually forms a hyper-positive idea of "being fully ready, possessing everything." *"And let endurance have its perfect result, so that you might be perfect and complete, lacking in nothing - possessing everything you need to handle life."* When you are mature and complete you do not lack.

In our lives we need to be prepared to meet the issues that inevitably come our way. If we are able to endure difficulties as they enter our life, then we will be able to display moral maturity and completeness in our life, revealing that we lack nothing; therefore demonstrating we are a fully functioning, mature believer. In his book, *The Third Man*, Graham Greene reflected on the purpose of pain nationally, but it is also true personally. *"In Italy for thirty years under the Borgias, they had warfare, terror, murder and bloodshed; but they also had Michelangelo, Leonardo da Vinci, and the Renaissance. In Switzerland, they had brotherly love, five hundred years of democracy and peace, and what did they produce, the Cuckoo clock."* Why do we suffer? Is it because there is no god or that he is a bad god or that he is not a sovereign god? To ask the question is to answer it. Times of testing and the accompanying pain are to help us mature as a man or woman of God. Pain is truly the gift nobody wants but everybody needs.

One of the leaders in the early church, Ireneas, coined the term "soul building" for the process that James is discussing. As we engage in life and its inevitable difficulties it is essential that we endure, for it is only then that we will not only survive, but succeed in our spiritual development. Let's be honest. We all want to mature and become complete, but we are not sure we want the hurt that accompanies and accomplishes it. But as Soren Kierkegaard said, "With the help of a thorn in my foot, I spring higher than anyone with sound feet."

James has taught his people that times of *testing produce Christian character*. Now he builds on this theme by adding that *testing provides Christian wisdom*. (James 1:5-11) If we are to become wise in the midst of trials and temptations, it is required that we desire and request from the Lord the divine Wisdom only He can provide. The concept of wisdom in the Old Testament has to do with the application of insight and knowledge. The New Testament term also carries this idea of the ability to see through a circumstance and apply the biblical knowledge to a life situation. Making wise decisions (applying biblical knowledge) in the midst of the normal disruptions of life is just that - "life"; for life is what happens after you plan. But when you find yourself in the midst of profound difficulties and personal disasters that seem to decimate your ability to function, that is when you need divine guidance to make discerning decisions. You need wisdom from above. And thank God He is eager to meet our needs; but it begins with us making a *request for the wisdom* we need. "But if any of you lacks wisdom, let him ask of God, who gives to all generously and without reproach, and it will be given to him." (James 1:5)

It is incumbent upon us that we seek the only wise God and request wisdom. This is an admission on our part that we cannot meet our own needs, that we need His word, and that we are willing to follow His way. In Proverbs 2 we see the same mindset.

> *My son, if you will <u>receive</u> my words And <u>treasure</u> my commandments within you,*
> *Make your ear <u>attentive</u> to wisdom, <u>Incline</u> your heart to understanding; For if you <u>cry</u> for discernment, <u>Lift</u> your voice for understanding; If you <u>seek</u> her as silver And <u>search</u> for her as for hidden treasures; Then you will <u>discern</u> the fear of the LORD And <u>discover</u> the knowledge of God. For the Lord <u>gives</u> wisdom; From His mouth come knowledge and understanding. He stores up sound wisdom for the upright; He is a shield to those who walk in integrity. Proverbs 2:1-7*

Do you see the point? Do you see the actions that we are to engage in as we seek divine guidance and wisdom?

The Purpose of Suffering

Also notice the Lord desires to give it to us, but we are to seek it from Him. It does not matter if we live in the ancient world of the first century or the modern world of the twenty-first century, the Lord desires that we understand while in the midst of trials and temptations that we need to seek divine guidance and wisdom from our heavenly Father. It is interesting to note the way James states the heart of God exhibited toward us in time of need. *"But if any of you lacks wisdom, let him ask of God, who gives to all generously and without reproach, and it will be given to him."* The original Greek text actually says; *if any of you lacks wisdom <u>ask from the giving God</u>*. This is crucial to understand in the midst of times of trial and temptation. The God we go to is "the giving God." That is part of His nature.

We know "God is Love." (I John 4:8) But what does it mean to "be loving" if not to be giving. James declares that when we go to God and ask for wisdom from Him we need to understand that it is part of who He is to give. *"God so loved the world that He gave His only begotten son..."* says it all does it not? Love gives and God is love, so God gives. Jesus said it so clearly that a child could understand. *"What father if his child asks for a piece of bread will give him a snake?"* As we say in the academic world, "duh." But notice also there is a *requirement for obtaining the wisdom* that we need and that God desires to give.

> *But he must ask in faith without any doubting, for the one who doubts, is like the surf of the sea, driven*

and tossed by the wind. For that man ought not to expect that he will receive anything from the Lord, being a double-minded man, unstable in all his ways. (James 1:6-8)

Now here is the problem. Make no mistake, the Lord wants us to ask and He desires to give; but we need to believe that He is, and believe in who He is. And that my friend, is a function of faith. It is not difficult to have faith in the good days, but add a few difficult circumstances and disheartening situations to your life and you discover that talk is cheap.

Faith is a topic we all like to talk about but often we find it difficult to exercise. James says faith is the key. Faith means to believe or trust. But our problem lies in the fact that instead of trusting we often doubt. When we doubt we are in two minds. It is not the same as not believing but it is to be in-between and operating in two minds. In a sense we are engaged in a debate.

Do you ever find yourself debating with God? Maybe you find yourself talking to yourself. It is not that you are hearing voices but you are in two mindsets. Part of you believes and the other part doubts. James describes this condition as being "a double minded man" or more accurately a "double souled man" or perhaps a two faced person. If you do not have faith then you do not really understand that God desires to give you the wisdom you need. And in fact, the Lord will not provide that which you desperately need in times of trial as long as you debate with Him.

The Purpose of Suffering

When you find yourself in the midst of a situation or circumstance that seems to just break you up inside and you do not know what to do; you need to know that our Lord desires to meet you in the midst of your greatest need and provide the wisdom you so desperately desire, so you can know what to do and how to do it.

When trials and tests come into our life, no matter what size or shape, we are to realize that they can actually produce proven character and also provide Christian wisdom if we request it from the Lord, meet His requirement of asking in faith, and refuse to debate and doubt Him.

James now gives us a picture or a reflection of what true biblical wisdom looks like. The reflection of wisdom is demonstrated in one of the most common issues in life: How do we view our lot in life? How do we view our social status and financial framework?

> *But the brother of humble circumstances is to glory in his high position; and the rich man is to glory in his humiliation, because like flowering grass he will pass away. For the sun rises with a scorching wind and withers the grass; and its flower falls off and the beauty of its appearance is destroyed; so too the rich man in the midst of his pursuits will fade away.* (James 1:10-11)

It is intriguing how James cuts to the heart of the issue. It does not matter if it is the first or the twenty-first century, social status and finances have always been the seminal thermometer to gauge a person's spiritual temperature. The first reflection of wisdom is described from the vantage point of the humble or poor person. If you are a wise person who lives in humble circumstances then your focus is on your high position in Jesus Christ. The truly important fact is your position with the Lord, not your bank account. Remember, you cannot take it with you. If on the other hand you have a high social status measured by wealth, a wise, rich person understands that the ultimate end of his fortune is that one day it will all burn up. In fact if you live for the dollar and all the material and social comforts it can bring to you, one day you will discover your life focus has been on the wrong thing. The Apostle Paul has a similar understanding as he states:

> *For the love of money is a root of all sorts of evil, and some by longing for it have wandered away from the faith, and pierced themselves with many a pang.* (1Timothy 6:10)
>
> *Instruct those who are rich in this present world not to be conceited or to fix their hope on the uncertainty of riches, but on God, who richly supplies us with all things to enjoy. Instruct them to do good, to be rich in good works, to be generous and ready to share, storing up for themselves the treasure of a good foundation for the future, so that they may take hold of that which is life indeed.* (1Timothy 6:17-19)

Jesus succinctly summarizes the truth as He always does by asking the essential and eternal question: *"What does it profit a man to gain the whole world and forfeit his soul?"* Answer---Nothing. What a terrible loss awaits those wealthy people who think their wealth is the key to life. James tells us that a truly wise, rich person understands that his treasure is a tool to be used not an idol to be worshiped for it is temporal in nature. There are many foolish Christians who have not learned this lesson. It takes a person of faith to believe in the world of the future, so as to live wisely in the world of today. (See Hebrews 2:5, 11:33; 12:28) Fortunately there are many wise, godly, Christians who have learned what wealth is to be used for and they invest it for the glory of God. But this takes wisdom. The wisdom from the Lord is that which can guide a person in the midst of life's most difficult circumstances and situations. It is a wisdom that will guide a person at either end of the social spectrum of life; either those who are of humble means or those of wealth or affluence.

Having revealed a reflection of what biblical wisdom looks like in this life, James now summarizes the final reason and result of enduring times of trials and testing in your life concerning your faith. The principle is succinctly stated:

> *Blessed is a man who perseveres under trial; for once he has been approved, he will receive the crown of life which the Lord has promised to those who love Him.* (James 1:12)

Let's unpack this climactic comment. Those who love the Lord, as evidenced by enduring under trials, shall be approved by receiving the crown of life and be blessed. Now the question that comes to my mind is: *"Is it worth it?"* It all depends on what the "approval" and reception of the "crown of life" and the "blessing" are talking about.

We all know there are offers in the marketplace that promise great benefits and tremendous rewards. But as the old adage says - *the devil is in the details.* When you see what it actually costs and what you actually get it is a whole new game. Like the great camera I was going to get for listening to a "short 90 minute presentation." We all have been there. Need I say more? But James is writing inspired scripture, revelation received from the mind of the Lord. So it is worth our time to determine what he is offering.

Each of us as believers in Jesus have been born again and are eternally safe and secure having received eternal life which can never be forfeited or lost. (John 3:16, 5:24, 6:40, and 10:28) However, trials and times of testing come into our life and although we cannot avoid their presence we can choose to respond in a way that is unpleasing to the Lord and try to escape. This is why James instructs us to allow them to work in our life. There is no option that difficulties will not come into our life, but there is the option of not responding well. But James is focusing on the reason we are to respond rightly. It has to do with the prize. As Helen Keller said:

*Character cannot be developed in ease and quiet.
Only through experience of trial and suffering
can the soul be strengthened, vision cleared,
ambition inspired, and success achieved.*

But not everyone is successful, nor does everyone win the race. (I Corinthians 9:24-27) Do not get me wrong. I did not say that a Christian can lose his salvation. That will not and cannot happen for salvation is an irrevocable gift from God. (Romans 4) But in the midst of trials we have a choice to make. We can either be faithful or we can doubt. We can receive the wisdom of God or we can debate with God. We can be blessed in our life or not. We can be found faithful and rewarded in the world of the future or forfeit the words of recognition from the Lord, "well done good and faithful servant." The choice is ours. We can either be crowned or crushed when trials come into our life.

There is coming a day when the Lord will evaluate our lives and reward every Christian for his or her life of service to King Jesus. This concept of reward for faithfulness is spoken about in almost all of the New Testament books. The Apostle Paul refers to it often as the Bema (Judgment) seat of Christ (I Corinthians 3-4; II Corinthians 5:9-10; Romans 14:10) or the Day of Christ (Philippians 2:16). The Apostle John talks about the "parousia" or the "coming" of Jesus and our desire to be found blameless. (I John 2:28; 2 John 8)

James refers to this idea of being rewarded for faithful service as being a person who can win the "crown of life" that is a "blessing" given to all who love the Lord as evidenced by enduring through times of testing. It might be hard for you to believe, but not every Christian will obey the Lord. In fact in times of testing and trial some Christians will not love the Lord. Yes, they are saved and secure eternally, but they will be scrutinized at the Bema seat.[11]

We must always understand that there is a difference between the **gift** and the **prize**. The gift of eternal life is free. The prize for living faithfully for the Lord must be earned. And faith is made perfect in trials. As St. Augustine said, "Greater joy is preceded by greater suffering." Our problem is that we view suffering as an infringement on our right to happiness. The truth is, suffering is the way to real happiness. Did not Jesus Himself prove this true and provide an example of the right attitude in suffering as He willingly experienced and endured suffering now so as to enjoy glory forever? James is simply telling us what he learned from His half-brother, the Lord of Glory, that the mindset, method, and motivation for surviving and succeeding in the midst of times of trials in this world is to have faith in the Lord now and live for the world of the future.

---

[11] [I Corinthians 3:15 - saved thru fire. Demas was guilty of loving the wrong world. (2 Timothy 4:10) Paul loved the right world. (2 Timothy 4:8)] As a result, the Lord Himself will evaluate our lives. Judgment will be fair and final, 2 Corinthians 5:9-10).

Conclusion

The secret to suffering successfully is to understand why the Lord has allowed times of testing into our life. This demands that we have a biblical mindset, operate under a biblical method, and always maintain a biblical motivation. Trials come into our life to make us better not bitter.

If we can know that God is and that He is the rewarder of those who trust Him, then we will begin to be able to allow trials in our life to perform their intended purpose in our life, and that is to make us mature and complete as fully functioning Christians. This can only come about as we trust God and have faith in His word, His will, and His way in our lives. If we are able to live for the world of the future and realize that **right now counts forever** we will be able to endure the present moment as we look to the eternal future with the King.

Only people of faith, people who see the invisible, will be able to do this. *We live life looking forward. We understand life looking backward. Faith means believing in advance that which only makes sense in reverse.* How is your faith?

> *"Hope is the thing with feathers that perches in the soul and sings the tune without the words and never stops at all."* ~ Emily Dickinson~

Suffering Successfully

Faith and the Silence of God

One must be a god to be able to tell successes from failures without making a mistake. ~Anton Chekhov~

It seems that for many of us who seek to follow the Lord Jesus we are often confronted with the danger of being overexposed and underdeveloped. This is often the case when we are dealing with faith and suffering. We have been exposed through the reading of many books and the hearing of many sermons on the topic, but we seem to be very under developed in our lives. This can be true both in the academic world as well as in the local church.

The doctrine of faith is vital. But a life of faithfulness is essential. We Christians often find it easier to talk a good game than to live one. As William James said, "Faith is either an acute fever or a dull habit." Which is it for you? Faith is like a tooth brush- everybody needs one, should use it often and by all means make sure you don't use anybody else's. At times in our spiritual journey faith is hard to come by and hazardous to live by. The often insightful Eli Wiesel has said, "For the unbeliever there are no answers; for the believer there are no questions." But that is not true, for I am a believer and I have questions, especially when life seems to be falling apart and spinning out of control. I feel more like the father with the little girl who was sick and Jesus said to him, "Now don't worry, only believe." The father replies with heartbreaking honesty, "Lord I believe, help my unbelief." I do not know about you but I find myself in times of suffering feeling like that father. I believe the Lord, that He is and that He has my best in mind. But the perplexing problems of the day cause me at some level to doubt. I find myself in two minds. All I can say is "Lord, I believe; help my unbelief."

If this is not difficult enough, let me add one additional element to our situation. Perhaps the most difficult challenge in the Christian life is to walk by faith in the midst of suffering and then sense that the Lord is not listening to us, not leading us. We can begin to wonder if He even likes us. It is hard to be faithful in suffering when God seems still and silent. What do you do when God seems silent? I have found that this perspective and perception often brings an abundance of confusion, an absence of confidence, and alienates me from His comfort. The fact is, when heaven seems so hushed I find myself horrified.

Perhaps you have had the disturbing experience of being alone and praying in a room. It's still and quiet as you speak, either verbally or within your soul to the Lord. But then in the midst of your prayer your eyes slowly open, your skin moistens, your body quivers and you ask that disturbing question that distracts your mind, disrupts your heart and disturbs your soul, "Is anybody here? Is God listening? Is He here for me? Is He even real?" At moments like this all we hear is the deafening silence of God. It is then you realize, maybe I really am all alone.

What do we do when God is silent in our lives? What are we to do when God is silent in the midst of unexplained suffering? What do we do when all of our dreams are shattered?

Unfortunately the options people opt for are predictable but not very profitable. First, many go into a state of *denial*. The result is to ignore the pain within and the silence from without and react with an overreaction that produces a false sense of boldness and bravado proclaiming, "I'm OK," "I don't hurt," "life is just great," "God is so good." It is true God is good but that is not actually what we are feeling. We become that backslapping, jovial, and inauthentic person seeking to deny his pain and the sense of silence from an absentee deity.

Second, for some the silence of God results in the desire to get *distracted* from the disinterest we sense we are experiencing from God. And so we get busy. We become the "Bionic Believer" or the "Supersonic Saint" working ourselves on the fast track, leading ourselves to both spiritual and physical burnout as we seek to find validation for our existence, hoping in the back of our mind and craving in the depth of our heart that God will speak to us, visit us, vanquish our doubts, validate His existence and answer our prayers. But a busy life can be a barren life and we must beware of trying to bargain or buy God's response.

The third response when denial and distraction refuse to stifle and suppress our pain is to *distort* reality and ourselves. We allow ourselves to become misdirected and misguided as we go after worthless things and in the process we become worth less. We become fearful not faithful when God is silent and in the process find ourselves experiencing a heaviness of heart and a hollowness of spirit.

To be sure (it goes without saying) God can seem silent when we are in sin. That is because we have moved away from Him. Scripture states unequivocally that God is light and in Him there is no darkness at all. If we say we are in fellowship with Him and we walk in the darkness we lie and do not practice the truth. (I John 1) But I am concerned for those of us who are walking toward God, dealing with our sin, and yet still sense His silence especially in the midst of our suffering that is not at all connected with our sin. In this situation God's silence is truly deafening.

Some write with delicate words, others with subtle silence. The Lord speaks to His people both in scripture and silence. Let's examine three snapshots of the silence of God as experienced through three personal vignettes of vastly diverse, distinct people displayed in scripture. The Lord desires that we understand truth. So, in the scripture we often see God "wrap the truth" around a person so it is incarnate and hard to miss the point. All three of these people find themselves in difficult times of suffering apart from being involved in sin, and yet experiencing the excruciating silence of God. [12]

The Silence of God and the Sinner

We begin with at best a secondary figure in the New Testament. She is not central to the story of the gospel - or is she? She is not a High Priest, Apostle, King or Roman Governor. She does not move the wheels of history and impact people of Israel. But we must give her due mention. Jesus described her faith as "great." And that must mean something.

> *And Jesus went away from there, and withdrew into the district of Tyre and Sidon.*
> *And behold, a Canaanite woman came out from that region, and began to cry out, saying, "Have mercy on me, O Lord, Son of David; my daughter is cruelly demon-possessed. (Mathew 15:21-22)*

First, notice what kind of person this woman is. As a woman she has no social standing in the world of the first century where Jewish men prayed daily, "thank God I am not a tax collector, a gentile dog, or a woman." But also notice this is a Syrophonecian, a Cannanite, in a word - a Gentile woman. Imagine her fear as both a woman and also as a Gentile as she seeks out the King of the Jews. She knows this dual stigma will

---

[12] I am indebted to Helmut Thielicke's sermon written in Nazi Germany, for these three snapshots. It is found in an edited collection of his sermons in a book: The Silence of God, Eerdmans Publishers, 1962.

illicit an attitude of chauvinism, bigotry, and a primal prejudice unrivaled in her day. So why in heaven's name come to Jesus? She must have heard something great about Him. She must have heard a rumor of His reputation, but then again there was the reality of the hatred of the Jews toward her people. But notice the woman's problem and perhaps a reason for her lack of hesitation. This mother knew that there was the fear of potential failure, for what if there was no answer for her child. After all, her daughter was not just sick but actually demon possessed - "cruelly" demon possessed. (Is there any other kind of demon possession?) It is no wonder that the woman cries out to Jesus recognizing His person and potential power, "Son of David have mercy on me." What more could this woman do?

The response of Jesus at this point is somewhat of a show stopper. It seems so incongruent with the "Jesus" we thought we knew from the pages of scripture. His words are so different and distinct from the familiar words, "God so loved the world that he gave His only begotten son..." Listen and see if you recognize Jesus in His words:

> *But He did not answer her a word. And His disciples came to Him and kept asking Him, saying, "Send her away, for she is shouting out after us."*
> (Matthew 15:23)

Total silence by Jesus; His lack of words leaves the woman wondering and His speechless silence leaves us all bewildered. The Savior is silent to this sufferer. It is hard to be in the face of

Jesus asking, pleading not for yourself but for another, perhaps in some sense an "innocent" child, and have Him silent. It is as if His compassion is empty, His concern extinguished.

There is something very wrong with this picture. Does He not care, is He not moved? But behind the silence of God is the **sovereignty** of God. The facts we see are true, but they are not all the facts.

The silence is quickly shattered and a total disparity in deportment is seen as the disciples enter the scene to rebuke the woman. They offer no mercy, there is no help coming from them. They seem to not even have heard the woman, yet we know they did for they demand that Jesus send the woman (and her daughter) away. It is interesting that the disciples' reason is one of fear but it is unclear what or who they are afraid of. They declare, "She is shouting out after us." Who is shouting, the woman or the little girl, who by the way is cruelly demon possessed? I suspect it is the demon through the girl that has frightened the disciples. However, imagine the fear of the woman when contemplating the demonic terror that is controlling her daughter? Nevertheless, she alone stands strong in her faith and goes toe to toe with Jesus.

Then Jesus responds a second time: *"But He answered and said I was sent only to the lost sheep of the house of Israel."* (Matthew 15:24) This time Jesus gives a theological reason for His rejection. It has to do with the one who sent Him. Jesus appeals to the Father as the one who sent Him and decided that

He is not to deal with this Gentile woman but only go to the lost sheep of the house of Israel. (See Matthew 10:5-6) This would never pass the political correctness test of our day. This is nothing other than the race card being played to silence the request of perhaps an illegal alien. But not everyone can take a hint even when it is the Son of God hinting. The woman begins a pensive but ultimately persuasive dialogue with Jesus.

> *But she came and began to bow down before Him, saying, "Lord, help me!"*
> *And He answered and said, "It is not good to take the children's bread and throw it to the dogs."*
> (Matthew 15:25-26)

Notice the persistence and the perspective of the woman. She is not run off by the first rebuff of Jesus or the rebuke of the disciples. In spite of the obvious rejection, the clear refusal, and stinging reprimand, she again approaches Jesus and appeals to His person and bows down to worship. Notice her request. In the original language it is communicated with an economy of language uttered in two words "help me." The more intense the feeling the fewer the words are needed.

Now at this point I must confess I am amazed and perplexed and I assume the woman was as well. Jesus has been known to call people names, but it is frequently reserved for those who deserve it. Here He actually calls this woman a dog. We must remember the proverbial and actual Jewish daily prayer of gratitude, "Thank god I am not a tax collector, a Gentile dog or a woman." Now she is two for three, but this woman is undaunted in her goal and undoubting in her faith no matter how impossible the facts appear or how personal her fear is.

> *But she said, "Yes, Lord; but even the dogs feed on the crumbs which fall from their masters' table." (Matthew 15:27)*

It's as if she is saying to Jesus, "You are right Lord, for you are the Messiah, the Son of David, the one who I came to see in hope against hope. But Lord... even the dogs....even the dogs." With this declaration *of proverbial home spun* wisdom and its spiritual implications Jesus cannot reject this lady any longer. For after all, did not the Savior come to save the world? (John 1:29, 3:16) Then Jesus answered and said to her, *"'O woman, your faith is great; be it done for you as you wish.'* And her daughter was healed at once." (Matthew 15:28) Jesus is caught in His compassion for this mother and daughter and I imagine His contempt for the demon. And with that, "it shall be done as you wish." Is there any wonder what the woman wished?

But do not miss the punch line of the story. "Woman, your faith is great." Mark it well; Jesus never said that to the disciples. Faith can only be called great when it is required because of a circumstantial crisis or a catastrophic situation. But faith is also great when it is maintained in the midst of the momentary silence of God. When we find ourselves in these cataclysmic times and experience the apparent silence of our

Savior we must persistently trust in God's personhood, His reputation, and His reality, even if He doesn't respond. In those times of partial blindness we must remember, all that I can see gives me confidence of what I cannot see.

That is the nature of faith. It is believing what you cannot see. It is believing the invisible. As the author of Hebrews declares *"Now faith is the assurance of things hoped for, the conviction of things not seen."* (Hebrews 11:1) Faith is trusting in that which you cannot prove, but believe to be true.

It is true that suffering can silence our sensitivity to God's presence. And at times it seems, and in fact it is true, that the Lord does not appear or act in ways that demonstrate His presence. But by faith we believe in Jesus whom we have not seen but through the eyes of faith we do see. Once again we can say, *"Lord, I believe, help my unbelief."*

It seems that often new Christians find an excitement in the presence of the Lord. Each day is a new and exciting expression of their new found experience and relationship with Jesus. But as the years go by, sometimes the freshness and excitement of our walk with the Lord is replaced with routine and sometimes rituals, many of them occurring on Sunday. That sense of vitality and excitement disappears. That may work when life is normal, but when life becomes abnormal and suffering begins to enter your life then the distance and silence of God can shatter your life.

The Silence of God and the Saint

The second snapshot concerning faith and the silence of God is wrapped in a primary figure of the Old Testament and a major figure in New Testament theology. Here we transition from an obscure Gentile woman in the New Testament to the most important Jewish man of the Old Testament. The multi-layered diversity in the juxtaposition of the two figures is significant but the theological truth is staggeringly similar.

The story of Abraham is proverbial and legendary; it is also historical and true. The specific situation is saturated in the promise of a son who will carry on the name and heritage of the Jewish race and fulfill the promise made by God to Abraham on many occasions. In Genesis 15 and 17 God has promised Abraham and Sarah a "son of promise." For God was to cut a covenant with Abraham with a son to be the proof of fulfillment. It is to be recalled that Abraham did not fully embrace this plan nor trust fully in God's promise, and at times sought to take matters into his own hands with devastating and disastrous effects. But finally after many years the promise came forth and Isaac was born. Everything looked like it was just fine and going according to plan. But then God spoke again to Abraham on one fateful night that could have changed all of history:

> *Now it came about after these things, that God tested Abraham, and said to him, "Abraham!" And he said, "Here I am." And He said, "Take now your son, your only son, whom you love, Isaac, and go to*

the land of Moriah; and offer him there as a burnt offering on one of the mountains of which I will tell you. (Genesis 22:1-2)

In modern society the idea of a burnt offering might be somewhat confusing. In this case it was simply an ancient death sentence. Abraham is to offer his son's life as a sacrifice. This is not as strange as it sounds to us modern readers of the Bible. In that day in the ancient near east, Abraham was well aware of the practice of child sacrifice, perhaps having been a worshiper of the moon deity of the day who demanded regular child sacrifice. He understood what God was asking. He just didn't see that this made sense in light of the fact that God said through Isaac shall you bring forth a nation. In light of God's prior promise His present pronouncement posed a serious problem for Abraham.

The situation happened as it always does on *one of those days:*

> *So Abraham rose early in the morning and saddled his donkey, and took two of his young men with him and Isaac his son; and he split wood for the burnt offering, and arose and went to the place of which God had told him. On the third day Abraham raised his eyes and saw the place from a distance.* (Genesis 22:3-4)

The story reveals two interesting events. First, Abraham got up early in the morning. Of course the last thing he wanted to do was meet Sarah at the door on his way out with Isaac, being asked some difficult questions like, "Where are you going and what are you and the boy going to do?" It is just so much easier to get up early. But the second piece of information is that it was a three day journey. For three days Abraham was stewing over a very strange command by the Lord. I imagine on the first day he might have asked himself, "Did I get the message right Lord? You know, Sarah might have let the ostrich stew get a little old - it tasted a little off- and it might have given me some crazy dreams. Lord, tell me again if this is really what you want." But there is no new revelation. He is simply obeying what God said the first time. Later, perhaps during the second day of the journey, taking a peek over his shoulder at his son, he might have been thinking, "Now wait a minute, Lord. Take a good look at that boy. He is a wonderful boy. He has been such a joy in my life. Lord, surely you do not mean for him to die. I'm sure you have more to tell me. Don't you?" But there is no new word from heaven. He is simply operating on the old word that God had revealed to him. I imagine on the third day out, going across the desert, Abraham let his donkey slide to the back of the group in order to gaze at his son and drink him up with his eyes and said, "Lord, now let me remind you this is the son that you promised, the one who would carry on the name and the family, you can't really take him from me now. Say something!" But there is no new word from God. In fact God's silence is deafening. It seems that a man can endure anything if he knows "why." But when there is no "why" it is almost unbearable. And without knowing "why," having arrived at the mountain, Abraham said these most incredible words:

> And Abraham said to his young men, "Stay here with the donkey, and I and the lad will go yonder; and we will worship and <u>return to you</u>."

There is a lot of hope in that statement. His faith is vocal even though God is silent.

> And Abraham took the wood of the burnt offering and laid it on Isaac his son, and he took in his hand the fire and the knife. So the two of them walked on together, And Isaac spoke to Abraham his father and said, "My father!" And he said, "Here I am, my son." And he said, "Behold, the fire and the wood, but where is the lamb for the burnt offering? "And Abraham said, "God will provide for Himself the lamb for the burnt offering, my son." So, the two of them walked on together. Then they came to the place of which God had told him; and Abraham built the altar there, and arranged the wood, and bound his son Isaac, and laid him on the altar on top of the wood. And Abraham stretched out his hand, and took the knife to slay his son. But the angel of the LORD called to him from heaven, and said, "Abraham, Abraham!" And he said, "Here I am." And he said, "Do not stretch out your hand against the lad, and do nothing to him; for now I know that you fear God, since you have not withheld your son, your only son, from Me. "Then Abraham raised his eyes and looked, and behold, behind him a ram caught in the thicket by his horns; and Abraham went and took the ram, and

> *offered him up for a burnt offering in the place of his son. And Abraham called the name of that place The LORD Will Provide, as it is said to this day, "In the mount of the LORD it will be provided. "Then the angel of the LORD called to Abraham a second time from heaven, and said, "By Myself I have sworn, declares the LORD, because you have done this thing, and have not withheld your son, your only son..."* (Genesis 22:5-16)

We all know this story but the principle for our spiritual life is at times elusive. However, it is simply this: when God is silent we need to trust in His pronouncements and His promises even if He doesn't tell us everything we desire to know. We must take Him at His word and trust Him in His ways. If He has provided us with His pronouncement then we must realize that He has spoken. He has not stuttered and we must operate on what He has told us, not on what we desire Him to tell us. It seems that Abraham understood this principle of patience as he made a simple theological conclusion: trust God's promise.

In Romans, Paul describes Abraham's declaration of trust in the initial idea of God's gracious gift of a child in light of the advanced age of both he and Sarah.

> *As it is written, "A FATHER OF MANY NATIONS HAVE I MADE YOU" in the presence of Him whom he believed, even God, who gives life to the dead and calls into being that which does not exist. In hope against hope he believed, so that he might*

> *become a father of many nations according to that which had been spoken, "SO SHALL YOUR DESCENDANTS BE." Without becoming weak in faith he contemplated his own body, now as good as dead since he was about a hundred years old, and the deadness of Sarah's womb; yet, with respect to the promise of God, he did not waver in unbelief but grew strong in faith, giving glory to God, and being fully assured that what God had promised, He was able also to perform.* (Romans 4:17-21)

But we are also told that in effect, Abraham made a wager - his only son. He doubled down on his confidence with God concerning the son of promise.

> *By faith Abraham, when he was tested, offered up Isaac, and he who had received the promises was offering up his only begotten son; it was he to whom it was said, "IN ISAAC YOUR DESCENDANTS SHALL BE CALLED."* <u>*He considered that God is able to raise people even from the dead*</u>, *from which he also received him back as a type.* (Hebrews 11:17-19)

Now that is quite a gamble except for the fact it was a sure thing. The fix was in because God was the one he was banking on. And when God is on your side then you better be all in. But it took faith in the person and promise of God to make the bet.

There are many times in our lives, when we would welcome a word from the Lord. In fact we do not think we can go on if we do not hear from Him. But what do we do when God gives no further prophecy, no clarifying proclamation, and no more scripture, but only silence in the midst of our anguish?

This seems to be an all too frequent experience of God's people. But that does not mean that the Lord will not provide. He will provide, but not necessarily on our time table. He is never ahead of time and never is behind. God will provide what is needed when needed in His time for His glory. Abraham believed that and declared it to his son in one of the most profound father son talks ever recorded: *"Where is the sacrifice my father?" "God will provide the sacrifice my son."* This is a simple, but far from simplistic question and answer. In fact, Abraham lived to see God's perfect timing and named the place *Jehova Jireha "The Lord will provide."* (Genesis 22:14)

Scripture is all one piece with theological themes running through its pages, written over centuries, coming together in perfect harmony. The Lord will provide the ultimate sacrifice on another hill of history, the skull hill called Golgotha. And it is to that later day that we look to see the third snapshot.

We have seen a mother and daughter, and a father and son. But now we look to the Father and the Son and once again see faith and the staggering silence of God. Here we see Jesus the cornerstone of the Old Testament and the centerpiece of the New Testament, experience the stunning silence of God as He offers a sacrifice for man, for it is ever true - The Lord will provide.

The Silence of God and the Savior

The idea of the image of God or the theology of the person of God in Christianity is centered on the reality of the tri-unity of God or the doctrine of the Trinity. We believe that God is one in His essence but three in his persons. The Bible describes the persons of the Godhead in many places. In 2 Corinthians 13 Paul declares, *"The grace of the Lord Jesus Christ, and the love of God, and the fellowship of the Holy Spirit, be with you all."* At the baptism of Jesus we see God the Father send God the Spirit to God the Son. One of the results of this is the essential truth of the importance of relationship and communication within the Godhead.

We know that the Father has communicated with the Son both from the baptism of Jesus, *"This is my beloved son in whom I am well pleased."* (Matthew 3:17) and the transfiguration, *"This is my beloved son listen to Him."* (Mark 9:7) We also know that the Son spoke to the Father as is evidenced in many of the times of prayer such as in the garden of Gethsemane.

But there was a singular moment in all recorded history, never before experienced in heaven or on earth when all communication seems to cease and all that is left between the Father and the Son is the silence of God. This was a dark day and the times were darker. Jesus has been betrayed by Judas, turned over by the Jewish leaders, tried and sentenced by Pilate, beaten and nailed to the cross by the Roman guards, and apparently deserted by God.

Jesus is agonizingly outstretched upon the instrument of His torture. He is alone in anguish and torment. As He is sensing alienation from man and abandonment by His Father, His cries of agony shot through the darkness like a thunderbolt. These cries were not simply from the physical pain He suffered, which were sufficiently severe to have killed numerous men before Him, but He also suffered the spiritual alienation from the guilt of the sin of the world. "He who knew no sin was made sin for us" (2 Corinthians 5:21). In the midst of this total anguish the Son of God cries out to His Father in the native Aramaic language *"Eli, Eli, Lama Sabachthani?" "My God, My God, why hast Thou forsaken Me?"* (Matthew 27:46)

If ever there was a moment in time for the miraculous power of God to be on display for all the world to hear and every person to see, now was that time. The backdrop of the wickedness of man and the wonder of God would have provided a perfect platform to validate the victory of the Son. But there is no proclamation from heaven. There is no further prophecy of scripture. Instead, there is only the silence of God and the laughter of men. But in the midst of the pain on the cross we must not miss the picture in the cross. Notice three thematic considerations as Jesus was hanging on the cross.

First, on the cross Jesus was naked and this was shameful. In the Jewish world this was the ultimate in shame and disgrace.

This ignominy and humiliation is evidenced as the soldiers of Rome are gambling for His clothing fulfilling the ancient psalm as it foretells of the crucifixion and shame for the Messiah.

> *They open wide their mouth at me, As a ravening and a roaring lion. I am poured out like water, And all my bones are out of joint; My heart is like wax; It is melted within me. My strength is dried up like a potsherd, And my tongue cleaves to my jaws; And You lay me in the dust of death. For dogs have surrounded me; A band of evildoers has encompassed me; They pierced my hands and my feet. I can count all my bones. They look, they stare at me; They divide my garments among them, And for my clothing they cast lots.* (Psalm 22:13-18)

Besides the prophetic voice from the historical past, it is not difficult to hear from the primordial past an echo of Adam and Eve hiding in the garden, their shame palpable both vertically and horizontally as they both hid from God and covered up from each other.

    The second theme is that the cross was an instrument of death, but also of shame and embarrassment. Not all prisoners were crucified. But when Rome wished to make a statement of disgrace and domination to any and all who would challenge her authority, the cross made just such a statement and was the final word. From the Old Testament perspective the cross, a tree, was a curse, and cursed was every man that hanged upon it. (Deuteronomy 21) And it is Paul, the consummate Old Testament Jewish theologian, author, and creator of the majority of the New Testament's Christian theology, who tells us that Jesus became a curse for us. *"Christ redeemed us from the curse of the Law, having become a curse for us-- for it is written, "CURSED IS EVERYONE WHO HANGS ON A TREE."* (Galatians 3:13) This curse echoes back to the garden where the ground and much that will grow from it is cursed due to the fall, sin, and rebellion against the words of God.

The third theme is seen as it ironically emerges from the crucifixion scene of Jesus. There He is naked, hanging upon that cursed cross, wearing a crown of thorns as a cursed criminal convicted for all mankind.

Again the Old Testament garden scene echoes in our ears, its presence almost palpable to our senses. The Genesis account speaks of the curse upon the ground forever impacting mankind manifested by thorns. Jesus in wearing this vicious crown of agony is in fact demonstrating His complete acceptance of the sin of the world. This was foretold by Isaiah as he spoke of the forthcoming suffering servant.

> *Surely our grief's He Himself bore, And our sorrows He carried; Yet we ourselves esteemed Him stricken, Smitten of God, and afflicted.*
> *But He was pierced through for our transgressions, He was crushed for our iniquities; The chastening for our well-being fell upon Him, And by His scourging we are healed.*
> *All of us like sheep have gone astray, Each of us has turned to his own way; But the LORD has caused the iniquity of us all To fall on Him.* (Isaiah 53:4-6)

> *But the LORD was pleased to crush Him, putting Him to grief; If He would render Himself as a guilt offering, He will see His offspring, He will prolong His days, And the good pleasure of the LORD will prosper in His hand.*
> *As a result of the anguish of His soul, He will see it and be satisfied; By His knowledge the Righteous One, My Servant, will justify the many, As He will bear their iniquities. Therefore, I will allot Him a portion with the great, And He will divide the booty with the strong; Because He poured out Himself to death, And was numbered with the transgressors; Yet He Himself bore the sin of many, And interceded for the transgressors.* (Isaiah 53:10-12)

It is as Saint Anselm said many years ago and we must realize today; *"Jesus did not come out of curiosity or personal need. The Father sent Him on an errand of mercy solely to accomplish our redemption."* The fact is Jesus was forsaken so that we would not be. *The life He lived qualified Him for the death He died. And the death He died qualified us for the life we live.* There is much hope for the sons of Adam and the daughters of Eve. But now He is on His cross with the crown of thorns and He cries out sensing the Silence of God, *"My God, My God why have you forsaken me?"* Was this the desperate cry of despair or defeat, or was this a dependence on the divine plan of God? Was Jesus asking "Why?" or "To what end?"

We need to notice three facts. First, this is not a random reaction to the situation of silence. In fact the Crucified One is praying a prayer, a Psalm foreshadowing the most monumental event of the miscarriage of justice in all of history: the crucifixion of the Son of God. Jesus took upon His lips the word of God, a liturgical prayer to lament His "God-forsakenness." And yet despite His distress and difficulty, He remained in contact with the Divine Creator.

As Thielieke observes:
Anyone who expresses his anguish and dread by making the word of God his witness is no longer groping and wandering along in some cosmic darkness, a deserted no man's land. He is praying in line with the patriarchs and the prophets, and with the people of God.

It is easy for us in the midst of pain and suffering and the silence of God to lose touch with the Father.

Second, this is not a response to the people and the human actions upon Him. Jesus is addressing God. In quoting the ancient Psalm, He is clear and perhaps comforted to know that it is His God He is calling upon, "MY God, MY God, why have YOU forsaken Me?"

The third observation is to notice this is not rejection of the Father by Jesus. Jesus is not rebelliously denouncing the divine majesty. For it is only a few moments later that He declares "Father" (not "God") into your hands I commit my spirit." (Luke 23:46) This combined cry of the savior, the son of God, is a cry from the utmost depths and the deepest darkness of despair.

As Thielicke again observes:

> *It involves passing through zones of alienation from men and from God that no man has ever endured. Nevertheless, in the midst of the suffering and sense of abandonment, as the darkness clutched Him from below, He reached out to the Father above. He was in a sense suspended in the abyss of nothingness but held in the majestic hands of God.*[13]

Jesus cried out like a tormented creature, but He lived with eternal confidence in the Father, even at a time when the circumstances made no sense and appeared to be utterly foolish. *"Father into thy hands I commit my spirit."* Even in the silence of God Jesus knew the plan and purposes of God. Jesus understood what the Apostle Paul would write in 2 Corinthians 5:21:

> *He made him who knew no sin to be sin on our behalf that we might become the righteousness of God.*

The crown of thorns first, then the crown of glory forever.

When God is silent in the midst of our suffering we must refocus from our problems and gaze upon His person and His proclamation, and also on His plans and purpose. Sometimes we don't fully understand what is going on in our life. The annoying afflictions seem to overwhelm us and cause us to cry out to what

---

[13] Helmut Thielicke, <u>Christ and the Meaning of Life</u> (Harper & Brothers, 1962) 45-46

feels like an empty room devoid of any presence of the divine. In those times in our lives we need to refrain from asking, "Why Lord?" and instead ask, "Lord, for what great purpose have you allowed this difficulty into my life?"

It is difficult to commit your spirit to the Lord when He seems so silent; as Blaise Pascal so accurately stated: *I see too much to doubt and too little to be sure.*

What we see is sometimes not enough to comfort us; so it is essential that we realize there is more that is not seen (than meets the eye). The story of the servant of Elisha in the midst of battle at Dothan makes the point as he saw a great army of horses and chariots surrounding the city and feared for his life as he warned Elisha, the man of God, saying, "Master what shall we do?" Elisha declared, "Do not fear for those with us are more than those against us." He then prayed to the Lord and said, "Lord open his eyes that he may see." The Lord opened his eyes and what he saw surrounding the city and on the mountain was the host of heaven, angelic warriors with horses and chariots of fire. (2 Kings 6:14-18) The battle was won, game over.

Often in our lives and in the midst of suffering, what we see and feel is real, but what we see is not all that is to be seen. God is the God of ends not just means. Sometimes His means are difficult, but when we can trust His person, His proclamation, and His plans, then we find supernatural company even in the midst of His silence and our suffering.

Jesus understood the person of God, His pronouncements, and His purpose; but He still felt the *sting of sin and the silence of the sovereign God*. Jesus also knew that God is the God of ends and that He will never leave us or forsake us. (Matthew 28:20; Hebrews 13:5)

Many of us may be experiencing excruciating pain and the deafening silence of God. It is described by St. John of the Cross as, "The Dark Night of the Soul." It comes in a variety of situations, but in all of its variations it can be devastating.

For some it is a marriage that is not all that you thought or wanted it to be. The marriage that started as an ideal has become an ordeal, and now you are looking for a new deal. Perhaps your kids are not where you wish they would be in their spiritual lives and for some reason God doesn't fix them. You pray but feel like your prayers are bouncing off the ceiling. For some in these troubled and uncertain financial times, money is a real issue. It seems that there is always too much month at the end of the money. For others, health issues or disabilities that come with age or life have caused you to cry out to the Lord but there is no answer.

The silence of God does not mean He is uninvolved or uninterested. What we see is not all there is to be seen. Behind the silence of God are higher thoughts. The question for us to consider is; "Do I believe God is and that He is the rewarder of those who diligently seek Him?" (Hebrews 11) If I do, then *"let us draw near to the throne of grace and receive in time of need."* (Hebrews 4:14)

As it has been said, "What we do when God is silent and we find ourselves in a crisis of faith always depends on whether we see our difficulties in light of God or God in the shadow of our difficulties." If our vision is right we can endure the silence of God and engage in service for God if we can say, "Into your hands I commit my spirit."

It is true as the old adage states:
> *We live life looking forward but we understand life looking backward. And Faith means believing in advance what only makes sense in reverse.*

This also is true:
> *We do not know what is coming into our lives. But we know who is coming; and He comes for us. And if we know He possesses the last hour, we do not need to fear the next minute.*[14]

And even if our Father is Silent, through faith we know that God is too kind ever to be cruel and too wise ever to make a mistake.

---

[14] Helmut Thielicke, <u>Christ and the Meaning of Life</u> (Harper & Brothers, 1962) 137

5

The Frame is Everything
Perspective in Suffering

*If I were to choose between pain and nothing
I would choose pain. ~ William Faulkner~*

I am told that in evaluating paintings the frame can make all the difference. The frame provides focus and perspective. It has been my experience that in the midst of suffering I often need to reframe my vision. I need a new perspective through which to perceive what is going on in my world.

    The ultimate example of such a reframing of perspective occurred in the life of Joseph. As you recall the story, his brothers, out of jealousy, threw him in a pit and left him for dead. They then lied to their father about what had happened. Next, God through his providential plans and power, delivered Joseph from the pit of death and placed him second in command over millions of lives in Egypt where he was perfectly positioned to save Israel from starvation and extinction. As the story concludes, the climax takes place as Joseph slowly and secretly reveals himself to his brothers. As the brothers and readers of the story throughout multiple millennia anxiously anticipate the conclusion of the story, we hear Joseph wisely announce to his guilt ridden brothers, *"You meant it for evil but God meant it for good."* (Genesis 50)

Now that is a radical reframing of reality if ever I heard one. As we read through the sacred scriptures we discover there are many times and many ways that the Lord guides men and women who are suffering and in pain, to reframe their view of what is happening and why it is happening. It is true that "the secret things belong to the Lord our God," (Deuteronomy 29:29) and we will never, this side of heaven, understand all of what happens in our lives or why it happens, just as Job experienced his troubles without understanding the ultimate realities. But the Lord does provide us with a picture and a grand perspective which if correctly perceived and received, allows us to reframe our world, especially when it is crashing down upon us. As F. B. Meyer has written, *"It is in proportion as we see God's will in the various events of life and surrender ourselves either to bear it or do it, that we shall find earth's bitter circumstances becoming sweet and its hard things easy."*

The Big Picture

Now for most of us the question in our minds is: If I am a Christian and bound for heaven, and heaven is such a glorious place of perfection, then why do I need to suffer now? I understand Catholics think no one is bad enough to go to hell and no one is good enough to go to heaven, so purgatory is a place to clean them up (at least most people). But, as a protestant and one who understands the doctrine of grace, I know that once I have received the free gift of eternal life by God's grace through faith in Jesus Christ the deal is done and I am eternally saved and everlastingly secure. So why do I need to suffer now?

In order to answer this perennial question we need to understand the biblical teaching about the theology of Salvation and Sanctification. Let me put it to you the way Jesus did. Jesus said, "I came that you might have life and life more abundantly." (John 10:10) In the natural world a person needs to be physically born. Once that takes place the person is to grow up both physically and socially, and experience and enjoy life to the fullest. In the spiritual realm it is no different. We need to be born again (Justification) and then we are to continue to grow in order to experience the fullness of God in our life now (Sanctification) and one day forever (Glorification).

The ultimate purpose and goal of the Apostle Paul's ministry is expressed as he declares, "*We proclaim Him, admonishing every man and teaching every man with all wisdom, so that we may present every man complete in Christ. For this purpose also I labor, striving according to His power, which mightily works within me."* (Colossians 1:28-29) Paul pronounces that his purpose is to present every person perfect or complete in Christ. This could have reference to only evangelism or it could also include edification and maturing in the Christian life. Perhaps it includes both, as does the Great Commission, as it declares that the goal is to "make disciples." The main verb in the sentence is "make disciples." The manner or means includes both evangelism, evidenced by the command to baptize and edification evidenced by the command to teach them all things I have commanded you. Both Jesus and Paul present a very clear and concise understanding of salvation and sanctification. We are to be born again - salvation. Then we are to grow up - through the teaching of the word of God and the ministry of the Spirit - sanctification. This is what I Peter 2:2 describes as *"long for the pure milk of the word that you may grow in respect to salvation."* Once you are born again you cannot be unborn. You are in the family. In theology we refer to this truth as "once saved, always saved." You are eternally secure. God in fact guarantees it in that He will preserve you to the end. As Jesus said:

> *My sheep hear My voice, and I know them, and they follow Me; and I give eternal life to them, and they*

shall never perish; and no one shall snatch them out of My hand." "My Father, who has given them to Me, is greater than all; and no one is able to snatch them out of the Father's hand." "I and the Father are one." (John 10:27-30)

This is great news. However there is a difference between being *"eternally secure"* and living a life of *"eternal significance."*

In order to comprehend the difference we must go one step farther in our theological understanding. We need to know a few essential facts about Eschatology, the study of end times. Salvation has to do with the past and sanctification has to do with growing spiritually in the present. Eschatology has to do with glorification in the world of the future.

The End Game

One of the better popular books to come out in the past decade on the "after life" is entitled *Heaven* by Randy Alcorn. The book provides some biblical answers to some real questions about eternity. There are a few ideas that are speculative and Randy admits that they are. But most of what he says about the afterlife is directly biblical and very helpful.

It is unfortunate that it is rare to have a good book on this topic. In the past many have been written that provide a glimpse concerning the world of the future.[15] But today people seem unclear about the future life for the Christian. Many people collapse the Millennial Kingdom, heaven, and the eternal state into an egalitarian event in which we all will simply float around in resurrected bodies or disembodied spirits, and have a good time forever. However, we need to know there is a bit more to the story. The ultimate end of history which is "His Story" is that paradise which was lost will one day be restored and regained. The devil - the god of this world - will relinquish the earth and the Kingdom of God will be rightfully reestablished throughout all creation. All that the Lord intended in the Garden of Eden will one day become a reality. This includes mankind ruling all of the created order for all time, just as it was meant to be in the garden from the beginning of time. In fact we will rule with King Jesus over the angels as we administrate the Kingdom of God throughout all of the created order. (Hebrews 2:5; Revelation 20:2-10) Jesus created it all and will inherit it all. (Hebrews 1:2-4) And we will have the privilege of the right to rule and reign with Him. In fact, Paul tells us we are to rule over the angels and the high role of ruler-ship belongs to the sons and daughters of Adam and Eve. (I Corinthians 6:3)

But it is important to know that this right to rule is given to

---

[15] *The Arena of Faith, From Eternity to Eternity, The Dawn of Redemption* and *The King of the Earth* all by Eric Sauer. Also see *The Greater Life and Work of Christ as Revealed in Scripture, Man, and Nature* by Alexander Patterson, and *Final Destiny* by Joseph Dillow.

The Frame is Everything

those who have earned it. You did not misunderstand; the right to rule the world of the future is for those who have endured and suffered for Christ and have triumphed and overcome the temptation, tests, and trials of this world. Jesus Himself, recorded by the Apostle John, made this promise to those who overcome. *"And he who overcomes, and he who keeps My deeds until the end, to him I will give authority over the nations."* (Revelation 2:26) The term for "overcomes" in the original language of the New Testament is "Nike." Yes, that is the name of the athletic shoe. But here it refers to the Greek goddess of victory, the daughter of Zeus himself, Nike. Jesus, in all seven of the letters in the book of Revelation found in chapters 2-3, issued a challenge to compete in this life to win the crown and be declared an "Overcomer" in the life to come in the world of the future.

It is important to remember that the "gift" of eternal life is free (Ephesians 2:8-9; Romans 4; John 4). The "prize" Jesus is offering is costly. It can cost a man or a woman their life. Listen to the clarion call to discipleship presented by Jesus in Luke 14.

> *Now great multitudes were going along with Him; and He turned and said to them, "If anyone comes to Me, and does not hate his own father and mother and wife and children and brothers and sisters, yes, and even his own life, he <u>cannot be My disciple</u>. "Whoever does not carry his own cross and come after <u>Me cannot be My disciple.</u> "For which one of*

you, when he wants to build a tower, does not first sit down and calculate the cost, to see if he has enough to complete it? Otherwise, when he has laid a foundation, and is not able to finish, all who observe it begin to ridicule him, saying, This man began to build and was not able to finish. Or what king, when he sets out to meet another king in battle, will not first sit down and take counsel whether he is strong enough with ten thousand men to encounter the one coming against him with twenty thousand? Or else, while the other is still far away, he sends a delegation and asks terms of peace. So therefore, <u>no one of you can be My disciple</u> who does not give up all his own possessions. (Luke 14:25-33)

It is important to realize the context, conditions, and consequences of the declaration of Jesus. This hardly looks like an offer of the free gift of eternal life. That is because it is not. Make no mistake - this is the clarion call to discipleship with Jesus. He demands <u>Unrivaled Commitment</u>, <u>Unceasing Cross-Bearing</u> and <u>Unreserved Cost</u>.[16] That is the price for living the Christian life. This is what it means to live as a disciple or follower of Jesus; and you had better count the cost.

It is also imperative that we understand the difference between the call, conditions, and consequences concerning the gift and the prize. Salvation as eternal life is focused on the free gift. Discipleship and sanctification are fixated on the costly prize.

---

[16] This triad is from a discussion with the late Howard Hendricks

Now the study of Eschatology or "end times" focuses on the role of Christians after death and for all eternity. As we have seen, there is a new and wonderful world that is called the Kingdom of God. It is a "Kingdom that cannot be shaken." (Hebrews 12:28) It will actually start on earth where Jesus will rule for a thousand years (Revelation 20) and then it will become an Eternal Kingdom forever and ever. (I Corinthians 15:22-28; 2 Peter 3) The question is, "What will we be doing then and what difference does that make now?" The simple answer is, "Right now counts forever." In the words of the Gladiator, Maximus, in the movie of the same name, "What we do in life echoes forth for all eternity." How true. And in light of this truth we should count the days and make the days count. The world of the future involves ruling with the King. This high honor and place of dignity is reserved for those who have proven their loyalty to the King in this life and will be rewarded in the life to come. The kingdom of God, both the Millennial and Eternal Kingdom is a place for great joy and service for Jesus Christ. All Christians will be in the Kingdom but only the faithful will rule. Consider the fact that we are all citizens of the United States of America. We enjoy the benefits and blessings of being a citizen, but only some of us rule in the government of the country. When a president is elected his or her first job is to select cabinet members to help rule in the administration of the country. I was not offended when the President did not call me for a cabinet post. Those positions are reserved for people who have worked loyally for the candidate and the president-elect. I never did, so I never got a call. The fact is I am not interested in serving in a government post that will last 4 years or 8 at most. But I am interested in serving in a government and a kingdom for 1,000 years and ruling with the Lord Jesus Christ for all eternity. That is very important to me.

The New Testament speaks boldly concerning the idea of being rewarded for faithful service. The Apostle Paul states in 2 Corinthians 5:9-10, "*I make it my ambition to be pleasing to Him for we must all appear before the judgment seat of Christ that each one may be recompensed according to his deeds done in the body whether good or bad.*" The word for "judgment seat" is the term "Bema." It was actually the place where Christ stood before Pilate (Matthew 27: 19) and the Apostle Paul stood before Festus (Acts.25:6) as judgment was rendered. The Apostle Paul picks up the concept and states that there is actually a "Bema seat of Christ" were each believer will have his life evaluated. The same idea is repeated in Romans 14:10-14:

> *But you, why do you judge your brother? Or you again, why do you regard your brother with contempt? For we shall all stand before the judgment seat of God. For it is written, "As I live, says the Lord, every knee shall bow to Me, And every tongue shall give praise to God." So then each one of us shall give account of himself to God.* (Romans 14:10-12)

As Jonathan Edwards reminds us:

> *There are different degrees of happiness and glory in heaven...The glory of the saints above will be in some proportion to their eminency in holiness and good works here [and patience through suffering is one of the foremost good works, cf. Romans 2:7]. Christ will reward all according to their works. He that gained ten pounds was made ruler over ten cities, and he that gained five pounds over five cities (Luke 19:17-19). "He that soweth sparingly, shall reap sparingly; and he that soweth bountifully shall reap also bountifully" (2 Corinthians 9:6). And the apostle Paul tells us that, as one star differs from another star in glory, so also it shall be in the resurrection of the dead (1 Corinthians 15:41). Christ tells us that he who gives a cup of cold water unto a disciple in the name of a disciple, shall in no wise lose his reward. But this could not be true, if a person should have no greater reward for doing many good works than if he did but few.*[17]

Peter is also mindful of this fact and uses it as a means of motivation for godliness. *"And if you address as Father the One who impartially judges according to each man's work, conduct yourselves in fear during the time of your stay upon earth."* (1 Peter 1:17) Every believer will one day stand before the Lord Jesus Christ and have his or her life examined by the Judge who without partiality and with total fairness, will determine the

---

[17] Jonathan Edwards, *The Works of Jonathan Edwards*, 2 vols. (Edinburgh: Banner of Truth, 1974), 2:902

value of the life we lived for the Lord. The Apostle Paul realized this truth and used it as motivation to serve the Lord Jesus.

> *Do you not know that those who run in a race all run, but only one receives the prize? Run in such a way that you may win. And everyone who competes in the games exercises self-control in all things. They then do it to receive a perishable wreath, but we an imperishable. Therefore I run in such a way, as not without aim; I box in such a way, as not beating the air; but I buffet my body and make it my slave, lest possibly, after I have preached to others, I myself should be disqualified.* (1 Corinthians 9:24-27)

Paul was not worried about losing eternal life nor was he concerned that he was not a Christian. However, knowing that a day of judgment was coming, a day for an evaluation of his life's work for the Lord, he hopes that he is found faithful by the Lord. The fact is Paul's hopes came true for as he makes his final declaration soon before his death:

> *I have fought the good fight I finished the course I have kept the faith. In the future there is laid up for me the crown of righteousness which the Lord the righteous judge will award to me on that day and not only to me but also to all who loved his appearing.* (II Timothy 4:7-8)

Paul certainly received a "*well done good and faithful servant. Enter into the joy of thy master.*"

This concept is also taught in the book of First John 2:28: *"And now little children abide in him so that when he appears we may have confidence and not shrink back in shame at his appearance."* Unfortunately when the Lord Jesus appears, there will be Christians who will have a sense of shame (Mark 8:38) for they will be doing or have done those things which they know displease Him. Although we are saved and eternally secure, there will come a time of final adjudication in which we will be evaluated and our eternal significance will be determined.

This significance finds itself manifested in the role of rulership that we receive in the kingdom of God. God's initial plan in the Garden of Eden was to allow Adam and Eve the right to rule over His creation. In the future that right will come to fruition when mankind will be judged and awarded the right to rule in the kingdom of God.

SO WHAT!

What does all of this have to do with suffering? What does this have to do with the difficulties I encounter in my life? It is simply this. *Suffering is the means the Lord uses to mature our faith in this life. Suffering is how the Lord trains us to trust Him, and be loyal to Him that we may honor and glorify Him.* You recall earlier we looked at James as he instructed the church in the midst of times of trials and testing:

> *Consider it all joy, my brethren, when you encounter various trials, knowing that the testing of your faith produces endurance. And let endurance have its perfect result, that you may be perfect and complete, lacking in nothing.* (James 1:2-4)

A rich and robust faith will be rewarded in our future life in the Kingdom of God. This is only accomplished as we are put in situations that allow us to strengthen and use our spiritual muscle and our faith. As Watchman Nee declared:

> *He who in time gets nearer to Christ crucified, will in eternity get nearest to Christ glorified. Indifference to Christ here cannot lead to intimacy there. Christ's future attitude toward men will be determined by men's present attitude towards him.*

The faith to endure today's difficulties is tied to the faith that believes in tomorrow's delights. Living faithfully in the midst of the horrors of today will result in experiencing the honors of tomorrow. To live effectively today you must have an education about what will happen tomorrow. The Scriptures clearly tell us that right now counts forever. What we sow we reap.

The concept of judgment or evaluation for the life we live is clearly anticipated in the Old Testament as Solomon, the wisest man of all the ancient world, is led by the Holy Spirit to tell us at the end of his book of wisdom: *"The conclusion, when all has been heard, is: fear God and keep His commandments, because this applies to every person; for God will bring every act to* judgment, everything which is hidden, whether it is good or evil." (Ecclesiastes 12:13-14)

Make no mistake; we are destined to rule in the world of the future in the Kingdom of God. (Hebrews 2:5, 12:28) Jesus will be King and we will serve Him as we administer His rule over all of His creation. (Revelation 2:26) This noble dignity, this high destiny, and these honorable duties are reserved for those who have been found worthy and have exhibited a fully orbed faith manifested in a life of faithfulness to the King in this life. **That kind of life can only be developed and displayed through acts of faith in the midst of suffering.**

Suffering is the gift no one wants but everyone needs if they wish to develop spiritual muscle and display the spiritual maturity that is worthy of reigning with Christ. Therefore, suffering allows our faith to fully function and manifest honor for the Lord now, and as a result He will honor us later in the world of the future.

This attitude is what leads to actions that please the Lord in the midst of suffering. Paul described this perspective and frame of reference by which to view the painful problems of this life. *"For momentary, light affliction is producing for us an eternal weight of glory far beyond all comparison, while we look not at the things which are seen, but at the things which are not seen; for the things which are seen are temporal, but the things which are not seen are eternal."* (2 Corinthians 4:17-18)

No one would suggest that Paul's life did not include

affliction. Just reflect on the list of his afflictions in 2 Corinthians 11:23-28:

> *Are they servants of Christ? (I speak as if insane) I more so; in far more labors, in far more imprisonments, beaten times without number, often in danger of death. Five times I received from the Jews thirty-nine lashes. Three times I was beaten with rods, once I was stoned, three times I was shipwrecked, a night and a day I have spent in the deep. I have been on frequent journeys, in dangers from rivers, dangers from robbers, dangers from my countrymen, dangers from the Gentiles, dangers in the city, dangers in the wilderness, dangers on the sea, dangers among false brethren; I have been in labor and hardship, through many sleepless nights, in hunger and thirst, often without food, in cold and exposure. Apart from such external things, there is the daily pressure upon me of concern for all the churches.*
> *(2 Corinthians 11:23-28)*

This is what Paul considers momentary and light affliction. It all depends on what you compare it with. For Paul that comparison of the temporal was with the eternal. In that case the difficulties he faced on earth were not worthy to be compared to the future that the Lord had for him. He follows a few verses later by reminding his readers and us as well:

> *Therefore also we have as our ambition, whether at home or absent, to be pleasing to Him. For we must all appear before the judgment seat of Christ, that*

> *each one may be recompensed for his deeds in the body, according to what he has done, whether good or bad."* (2 Corinthians 5:9-10)

Paul reminds his readers and himself, I imagine, that one day there will be a final evaluation. The examination is not to determine if a person is saved. Salvation is accomplished by one act of faith that appropriates the water of life-the gift of eternal life. As G.H Lang has said, *"The water of life is not acquired by the process of fighting a life-long battle and conquering at last. It is a free gift, imparting spiritual life to the spiritually dead."* But now that Paul had received the free gift of eternal life and was eternally secure he desired to be found faithful and become eternally significant. And this was accomplished by those who had lived a life of faith in the midst of suffering for Christ.

As Paul looked at life he realized, *"For I consider that the sufferings of this present time are not worthy to be compared with the glory that is to be revealed to us."* (Romans 8:18) It is all in one's perspective. It is how you choose to frame your life that counts. So, count the days and make the days count because right now counts forever!

Vision is Everything

The Lord often wraps truth around a person so we can better understand the truth. Consider the mindset of two of the great Old Testament saints, fathers in the faith, heroes of history and their perspective on how and why they lived their lives. First we look at the mindset of Abraham. Here was the Old Testament patriarch and a man of faith.

> *By faith Abraham, when he was called, obeyed by going out to a place which he was to receive for an inheritance; and he went out, not knowing where he was going. By faith he lived as an alien in the land of promise, as in a foreign land, dwelling in tents with Isaac and Jacob, fellow heirs of the same promise; for he was looking for the city which has foundations, whose architect and builder is God.* (Hebrews 11:8-10)

Notice where Abraham was "looking" and where his focus was; it was not on the difficulty of the present world nor the riches it might provide. He was fixated on the reality of the future world and a city that was to be built by God. Now consider Moses a few verses later.

> *By faith Moses, when he had grown up, refused to be called the son of Pharaoh's daughter; choosing rather to endure ill-treatment with the people of God, than to enjoy the passing pleasures of sin; considering the reproach of Christ greater riches than the treasures of Egypt; for he was looking to the reward. By faith he left Egypt, not fearing the wrath of the king; for he endured, as seeing Him who is unseen.* (Hebrews 11:24-27)

Notice what he chose and why he chose it. He chose to suffer in the present because he was looking to the reward of the future. He decided to suffer and endure difficulty now so as to delight in the world of the future. Moses realized there was, as there always is, a choice to be made in the midst of the turmoil of life. But notice also not only what he chose and why he chose it but who he saw. He saw Him who was unseen. He exercised faith; and faith believes in the invisible.

> *The only way to endure difficulty in the present is to look past that which is good and toward that which is great. In the midst of suffering we must discern and desire the greatest things, set eternity against time, and choose rather to be great in the presence of God than to have the greatest share of worldly pleasure while we live.* ~ Watchman Nee ~

Moses had such a perception, to understand the reality of the present world with all that it promised and chose to live for the reality of the prize of the future world. And this is often the choice we must make. Do we live for the present temporal world or for the eternal world of the future?

We must keep our eye on the prize. The prize is the restoration of the Kingdom of God ruled by King Jesus. This is the transformation of paradise ruined to paradise restored. In this kingdom the Lord Jesus will rule and reign and He will have companions, partners to rule with Him just as He promised Adam and Eve the right to rule and have dominion. They failed but the second Adam, Jesus, has won the victory; and as a prize the redeemed will rule with Him over the entire universe which He created. (I Corinthians 6:2-3; Hebrews 1:2-3) Those who are bestowed the right to rule are those who remain faithful in the midst of suffering in this life. It is given to those who did not fail in their faith but entrusted themselves to the faithful creator.

In the midst of suffering it is often difficult to make such wise decisions as Moses and Abraham made, but make them they did and they are provided as mentors for us to follow in the midst of suffering. It is in the midst of suffering in this life that we must understand that suffering is forging a prize and reward for the future in the city of God and the kingdom of God. Of course this takes faith and in fact a strong faith that is able to see the unseen and believe in the invisible. In fact, sometimes, and especially in the midst of suffering, faith means believing in advance that which only makes sense in reverse.

The Messiah's Model

It should not surprise us that Jesus understood this truth and shared its perspective. After all He is the coming King and it is His Kingdom. But we must remember that He went through a time of testing. It is also imperative to note that we, as He, learn through the things we suffer. The Book of Hebrews has at its central point the fact that Jesus is the coming King and that He was vocationally prepared and perfected for His role as ruler through His experience of suffering. *"Although He was a Son, He learned obedience from the things which He suffered. And having been made perfect, He became to all those who obey*

The Frame is Everything

Him the source of eternal salvation." (Hebrews 5:8-9) The idea of perfection does not imply that He was lacking morally or that He had sinned. It has to do with the demonstration of His exquisite qualification to be the future ruler which was demonstrated through His present suffering. As such it is only natural that He is given to the Church as the perfect example to emulate as the writer of Hebrews exhorts his audience in the midst of their sufferings.

> *Therefore, since we have so great a cloud of witnesses surrounding us, let us also lay aside every encumbrance, and the sin which so easily entangles us, and let us run with endurance the race that is set before us, <u>fixing our eyes on Jesus</u>, the author and perfecter of faith, who for the joy set before Him endured the cross, despising the shame, and has sat down at the right hand of the throne of God. For consider Him who has endured such hostility by sinners against Himself, so that you may not grow weary and lose heart.* (Hebrews 12:1-3)

And there it is! Fix your eyes on who Jesus is and what Jesus did. Focus not on the suffering, but the purpose of the suffering. Focus not on the actual pain of the temporal moment, but the eternal plan of God for the forever future. A choice must be made. Will we choose to suffer now to be exalted later or allow our faith to falter and forfeit the reward of the future?

The old hymn had it right: *"Turn your eyes upon Jesus and look full in his wonderful face and the things of this world will grow strangely dim in the light of his glory and grace."*

Perspective is everything. Listen to the eternal frame of reference that G.H. Lang provides for those who are encountering difficulty in this life:

> *In the purpose of God, the world (oikoumene) of the future has not been put under the control of angels, but of men. This is a key thought, the resolving of many obscurities and perplexities which hinder believers from grasping the exact significance of the plans of God and the final and highest outcome of redemption. It is the key to some present enigmas. At present, God is not saving the human race entire and its affairs corporate, but is selecting from it the company that are to rule the universe, superseding the existing government. He is preparing for a complete reorganizing of His entire empire, and is giving to these future rulers the severe training which is indispensable to fitting them for such responsible duties and high dignities. The gospel has not failed, but is fulfilling the purpose God plainly announced, though not the end that many preachers have mistakenly proposed, namely the conversion of the whole race. That general and desirable betterment of this sin cursed earth is in the plans of God, but falls for accomplishment in the next period of the divine programme, not in this age. There is manifest wisdom in a great Leader first training a body of efficient subordinates before seeking to reorganize society at large.*

The goal of the Christian life is to become conformed to the image of Christ. We call this sanctification. The reason is that we might glorify Christ now and serve Him for all eternity. We believers in Jesus endure present momentary light affliction so we might be trained and prepared to serve Jesus in the world of the future. Suffering has the potential of sanctifying us which results in glory and honor in the kingdom of God. As the Apostle John declares, *"And he who overcomes, and he who keeps My deeds until the end, to him I will give authority over the nations and he shall rule them with a rod of iron, as the vessels of the potter are broken to pieces, as I also have received authority from My Father..."* (Revelation 2:26-27)

It should not surprise us that suffering is to precede the glory to follow for it was just so in the life of Jesus as the Apostle Peter makes clear:

> *As to this salvation, the prophets who prophesied of the grace that would come to you made careful search and inquiry, seeking to know what person or time the Spirit of Christ within them was indicating as He predicted the sufferings of Christ and the glories to follow.* (1Peter 1:10-11)

Do you see it; suffering now, but glory to follow? This is the divine paradigm. We must realize that in the plan of God it is His will for us to be matured and perfected as His children. This is accomplished through training of the highest order which includes the essential ingredient of suffering in this world that we might inherit the world of the future.

A Strategy

"In the world you will have tribulation. But do not fear I have overcome the world." The words of Jesus provide the ultimate frame of reference and perspective to living successfully in this life. We will suffer. Take it by faith, Job was right. *"For man is born for trouble, as sparks fly upward.* (Job 5:7) But thank God that in His marvelous plan He has provided to make known to us the ultimate purpose of pain that comes upon us; and that is to prepare us for the ruler-ship of the world to come.

I know there are times when we feel like forgetting the world of the future in light of the pain in the present, especially when it seems to be so pervasive and permanent. But this is where we must manifest a mature faith; one trusting that God is too kind to be cruel and too wise ever to make a mistake. At times we need friends and family to help us think right and provide the prayer and encouragement that we ourselves feel is not within us. This teamwork is simply how the body of Christ is to work, for as Paul tells us in 2 Corinthians:

> *Blessed be the God and Father of our Lord Jesus Christ, the Father of mercies and God of all comfort; who comforts us in all our affliction so that we may be able to comfort those who are in any affliction with the comfort with which we*

> *ourselves are comforted by God. For just as the sufferings of Christ are ours in abundance, so also our comfort is abundant through Christ." But if we are afflicted, it is for your comfort and salvation; or if we are comforted, it is for your comfort, which is effective in the patient enduring of the same sufferings which we also suffer; and our hope for you is firmly grounded, knowing that as you are sharers of our sufferings, so also you are sharers of our comfort. For we do not want you to be unaware, brethren, of our affliction which came to us in Asia, that we were burdened excessively, beyond our strength, so that we despaired even of life; indeed, we had the sentence of death within ourselves in order that we should not trust in ourselves, but in God who raises the dead; who delivered us from so great a peril of death, and will deliver us, He on whom we have set our hope. And He will yet deliver us, you also joining in helping us through your prayers, that thanks may be given by many persons on our behalf for the favor bestowed upon us through the prayers of many.*
> (2 Corinthians 1:3-11)

Now, you might think you are having a bad day, a bad life. Paul's life as a Christian was a huge mess but it actually provides the backdrop for a beautiful message to the Church.

Notice first that Paul declares our "God is the Father of mercies and the God of all comfort." He is personal as our heavenly Father and powerful as the One who possesses the power to comfort us. But then Paul declares that the reason for suffering is in one sense to allow us to experience the comfort of

God so that we can pass it on to others who suffer as we do. This is true body life in action. We are not simply individuals lost in our pain. We are a part of the body of Christ, unified under one Lord, one faith, one baptism, and one God and Father of all. We are united, ready to serve one another in the midst of pain and suffering in order to manifest the power and love of God which comforts us, and convinces us that God is good and worthy of being glorified even in the midst of our trials and tribulations. What a testimony of the power of God experienced in the body of Christ. But there is one other benefit. As we learn to live and suffer together we make visible the invisible Christ to a lost and dying world.

There is an old Latin phrase, *solvitur ambulando*[18], which means, *"It is solved by walking."* The questions concerning the problem of evil and the reality of pain and suffering in this life are not simply answered by a definition or description in a book or lecture on life. These questions are understood and resolved by living them out through one's life in relationship with God. *"It is solved by walking."* The answer to this riddle of life can only be seen in the midst of suffering in the real world.

The words and works of the Lord Jesus provide both a model and a method for us to follow. The Apostles Paul and Peter provided a theology of suffering forged in the crucible of life which they lived right up to the point of their death and into

---

[18] Often attributed to Diogenes of Sinope, 412 BCE.

eternal life. And it is in their lives which led to death that we see and understand the truth: *"If you want to save your life you will lose it, but if you lose your life for My sake you will save it."* This enigmatic saying uttered by Jesus to His disciples on many occasions perhaps will provide us with a key to suffering successfully. It is on this divine axiom that we must focus our attention.

Salvation of the Soul

Nothing is more important for us to see in the light of the Word of God than sickness and suffering.
~O. Hallesby~

The right optic can create real optimism. But through what lens must we focus to perceive the proper view of reality to guide us in the midst of a life that includes suffering? It is true that, "Life is hard and then you die." But it is also true that when we die, then we live ... forever!

Jesus made many pronouncements in the form of axioms, aphorisms, and proverbial statements. But perhaps the most inscrutable and inexplicable truism was one He said on a variety of occasions to His disciples and one we must understand if we desire to understand what life is about and how to live it. We must understand the *Problem* of evil with the results of sin and suffering. Sometimes the two are directly connected and other times they are only indirectly connected as a consequence of living in a fallen and finite world. It is sin that has caused the cosmic struggle (Romans 8:19-22) in which all of creation groans and awaits the provision of the savior of all the creation. The *Provision* of the Son of God, accessed through faith, provides eternal life for every man or woman who will receive the free gift of eternal life. We have seen the *Perspective* we as Christians must have as we live out our days in this temporal world. We must focus our minds on the eternal world of the future knowing that right now counts forever.

It is imperative that we understand there is a *Promise* for those who live a life of loyalty and faithfulness to Jesus in the midst of suffering and sorrow, and who encounter difficulty, distress, and deprivation. The truth is we can often feel like we are living a life of desperation. As a result, it seems like we are in a sense, "losing our life." And here is where we find the promise of Jesus. *"If you save your life you will lose it but if you lose your life you will save it."* What possibly can this mean and what possible difference can it make for me in the midst of my own personal pain? I know He has the power to eradicate my suffering and difficulty. Yet, I know He has chosen not to do so. I know He is personally good, but my life seems to be going so bad. So what does this illogical and nonsensical proclamation mean: *"If you save your life you will lose it; if you lose it you will save it"?* If it were anyone but Jesus we might dismiss it as some absurd and ludicrous pronouncement. But it is Jesus Himself who proclaims it so we must investigate to see if its meaning could perhaps provide some insight as to why and how to live our life in the midst of the unmapped territory of suffering.

A Hard Saying: A Consideration

This statement is found in all of the synoptic gospels. (Matthew 10, 16, Mark 8, and Luke 9) We will focus on the final use found in Matthew 16.

> *From that time Jesus Christ began to show His disciples that He must go to Jerusalem, and suffer many things from the elders and chief priests and scribes, and be killed, and be raised up on the third day. And Peter took Him aside and began to rebuke Him, saying, "God forbid it, Lord! This shall never happen to You." But He turned and said to Peter, "Get behind Me, Satan! You are a stumbling block to Me; for you are not setting your mind on God's interests, but man's." Then Jesus said to His disciples, "If anyone wishes to come after Me, let him deny himself, and take up his cross, and follow Me. "For whoever wishes to save his life shall lose it; but whoever loses his life for My sake shall find it. "For what will a man be profited, if he gains the whole world, and forfeits his soul? Or what will a man give in exchange for his soul? "For the Son of Man is going to come in the glory of His Father with His angels; and will then recompense every man according to his deeds. (Matthew 16:21-27)*

Perhaps you have read this passage of scripture or heard a sermon as to its meaning. Often it is interpreted and understood as a call to conversion and it is used much like John 3:16 to present the gospel. But this perspective produces a problem in that the freeness of the gospel is compromised. If we are honest, what part of this looks like a *free gift*? The conditions are clearly spelled out. In fact, in the parallel account presented in Luke's gospel the conditionality of the invitation is even more clear that this is anything <u>but</u> a free gift, for the requirements include "daily" sacrifice of one's life as a condition to be saved.

> *And He was saying to them all, "If anyone wishes to come after Me, let him deny himself, and take up his cross <u>daily</u>, and <u>follow</u> Me. (Luke 9:23)*

Perhaps this is not actually a gospel invitation at all, but instead it is a clarion call to discipleship.

The account in Matthew provides us with some very important background and circumstances we need to understand if we are to interpret this passage correctly.

> *Now when Jesus came into the district of Caesarea Philippi, He began asking His disciples, saying, "Who do people say that the Son of Man is?" And they said, "Some say John the Baptist; and others, Elijah; but still others, Jeremiah, or one of the prophets." He said to them, "But who do you say that I am?" And Simon Peter answered and said, "Thou art the Christ, the Son of the living God." And Jesus answered and said to him, "Blessed are you, Simon Barjona, because flesh and blood did not reveal this to you, but My Father who is in heaven.*

> *"And I also say to you that you are Peter, and upon this rock I will build My church; and the gates of Hades shall not overpower it. "I will give you the keys of the kingdom of heaven; and whatever you shall bind on earth shall be bound in heaven, and whatever you shall loose on earth shall be loosed in heaven." Then He warned the disciples that they should tell no one that He was the Christ. From that time Jesus Christ began to show His disciples that He must go to Jerusalem, and suffer many things from the elders and chief priests and scribes, and be killed, and be raised up on the third day. And Peter took Him aside and began to rebuke Him, saying, "God forbid it, Lord! This shall never happen to You." But He turned and said to Peter, "Get behind Me, Satan! You are a stumbling block to Me; for you are not setting your mind on God's interests, but man's.* (Matthew 16:13-23)

First, consider the context. Jesus is speaking to the disciples about His identity. Peter makes the definitive and divine declaration that Jesus is the Christ, the son of the living God. Jesus gives His divine approval and then informs the twelve disciples that He is going to the cross and He is going to die. Peter responds by telling Him this is not to be. The Lord clarifies that Peter is now operating from the wrong viewpoint. In fact he is seeing things from the devil's perspective and this is just moments after he made such a tremendous pronouncement that Jesus is the Christ, the son of God. Peter's divinely sourced declaration has devolved into a conclusion sourced in the devil. It appears that a lot can change in a few moments.

Second, consider the conditions required. Jesus is speaking to His disciples, saved individuals, and Peter specifically, who has just declared the identity of Jesus as the son of God, having been given this information by God Himself. The invitation from Jesus to his apostles is to come and die. Jesus had just told them all He was going to die at the hands of the chief priest, the scribes, and rulers. He is inviting His own disciples to come and do the same.

The prospect of a cross was a clear picture of the government endorsed penalty of painful capital punishment. It was reserved for criminals who were used by Rome to make a statement about its total dominance and control in all matters related to life in the empire. The special form of punishment and propaganda was both brutal and memorable. Jesus was asking His disciples to consider joining Him. Peter rebukes the Lord, saying this was not a good idea and that this was not God's idea. Jesus declared Peter's viewpoint was in fact demonic.

The passage in Luke softens and yet deepens the request and the requirement saying if it is not actual physical death, then it involved a "daily" attitude and action of "follow Me." But this total commitment to Jesus was the cost of discipleship and was certainly not the free gift of eternal life. The nature of the command and the price to be contemplated was to claim the entirety of a person's life which would or could require their death.

Third, notice the consequences. If Jesus' statements were taken entirely literally they would sound like nonsense. How can a person actually save their life physically resulting in losing it physically? How can a person lose their physical life and result in saving it physically?

On this level, words seem to confuse their meaning and lose their significance. However, scripture is also literature and often times we must understand how words are being used from a literary perspective.

We must begin by first understanding the scope of the meaning of the terms Jesus utilizes to make such a provocative statement. Second, we must understand the literary container encasing the theological comment made by Jesus.

The terms utilized are critical as we consider the meaning of the text. The term "save or saved" is often automatically assumed to mean "we are going to heaven." For example, "I got saved at the Billy Graham crusade and am bound for heaven." This past action, "saved," also has a future result, going to heaven. Passages such as Titus 3:3-6 and Ephesians 2:8-9 refer to this aspect of salvation. However, Christians who are saved eternally (justified before God) still grow in their salvation, which is actually referring to sanctification or maturing in the Christian life. As both Peter and Paul declare:

> *Like newborn babes, long for the pure milk of the word, that by it you may grow in respect to salvation...* (1Peter 2:2)
>
> *So then, my beloved, just as you have always obeyed, not as in my presence only, but now much more in my absence, work out your salvation with fear and trembling* (Philippians 2:12)

The term "salvation" can also refer to Messianic rule with Jesus in the Millennial Kingdom of God that is given to those who are found to be faithful disciples of Jesus. (Hebrews 1:14, 2:3; Psalm 98:2-3, 9) This appears to be connected with the concept of the Bema seat. (2 Corinthians 5:9-10; Romans 14:10; I John 2:28)

The term "salvation" can also have the meaning of being saved or delivered physically, as in James 5:15 and Acts 27:31. Hence, the term has a field of meaning that can refer to being saved to heaven or being delivered from physical harm on earth. (The Psalms often use the phrase "deliver me" with the meaning being rescue me or save me.) It can be used in the past, present, or future referring to those who are saved, being saved, or will be saved. As Lewis Sperry Chafer said:

> *We as Christians have been saved from the penalty of sin in our justification, and are being saved from the power of sin by sanctification and one day will be saved from the very presence of sin in glorification.*

Praise be to God for His glorious grace.[19]

The other concept we must understand is the term "soul." The term in both the Old Testament and the New Testament has a large field of meaning. It can refer to the physical or material person. (Genesis 2:7; Matthew 2:20, 20:28; John 10:11, 17; Acts 20:10) The term can also be defined as the person himself or as selfhood (Deuteronomy 10:22; Joshua 20:3) or as the inner person (2 Corinthians 12:15; 2 Peter 2:8; Hebrews 10:38) and perhaps the immaterial part of a person. (Hebrews 4:12) The Greek term is a form of the word from which we derive the term psychology or the study of the psyche or soul. In the ancient Greek culture the term had the idea of the immaterial part of a person that was a "spirit-soul-ghost-like" entity, but this concept came from Plato not the Old or New Testament scriptures. However, the "soul" could be used to represent that part of a person having the capacity to enjoy or feel emotions such as joy, sorrow, love, hate, bitterness, and pleasure. (Psalm 35:9; Isaiah 9:10; Song of Solomon 1:7; Psalm 11:5; Joshua 27:2; Luke 12:13-20)

Having examined the terms "salvation" and "soul" utilized by Jesus, it is now imperative that we understand the literary container in Matthew's account of the Lord's theologically important statement, *"If you want to save your life you will lose it but if you lose your life you will save it."*

There are a variety of instances and uses of figurative

---

[19] Lewis Sperry Chafer, *Salvation* (Kregel Publishing, 1991) 15

language in the sacred scriptures. We certainly do not take it literally when we say, "The eyes of the Lord are upon the righteous..." or "the right arm of the Lord is lifted high" to mean that God has actual literal eyes or arms. But we do take it to be a figure of speech similar to what we find in all great literature. Scripture can have a literary quality and still convey a literal meaning through the use of figures of speech.

One tool or literary device of figurative language is the use of metonymy, where the subject being considered is replaced by something pertaining to it as the container for the thing contained or the thing signified for a sign. If we were to say, "The White House said today that the economic reports will be announced next week." We clearly understand the meaning and function of the term "White House." We do not think that houses with white paint speak audibly. It is representing something contained inside of it such as the Press Secretary or the President himself.

If the soul is seen as functioning as a metonymy of subject, then the logic of the saying is understood. The soul stands for or represents an ability or aspect. If the use of the term soul is to represent the part or aspect of a person which experiences the joys and sorrows of earthly life, then the words of Jesus become understandable and theologically meaningful. As a metonymy of subject the soul is substituted for the thing connected with it. If the soul is the part of man that enjoys the joys and pleasures of life, the soul is substituted for the joys and pleasures of life. The logic of the statement with the use of metonymy implies that the person who saves himself by enjoying the passing pleasures of this age to the fullest measure will in fact forfeit or lose their soul because he or she will actually lose the ability to enjoy those pleasures in the age to come.

However, the opposite is also true. The person who loses his soul in this age by giving up the pleasures of it for the sake of Christ, and endures the difficulties of this life as a faithful follower, that person will in actual fact save his soul and have the ability to fully enjoy the pleasures of the age to come. Whatever a person preserves in this age he will in fact lose in the age to come. But that which a person determines to give up in this age, they will receive back in the world to come. The salvation of the soul functions as a reward for individuals who are willing to follow Christ and give up the passing pleasures of this age for the age of the future.[20]

We are not talking about losing one's eternal salvation or forfeiting eternal life. Eternal life is eternal. (John 5:24, 10:28-29) We are talking about the loss of reward earned for faithful service to Christ in this life which will be experienced in the life to come. *Eternal security* is a positional status that cannot be lost. *Eternal significance* for service in the kingdom of God is a potential reality that must be found. This reminds us of the discussion concerning the Bema seat of Christ and the right

---

[20] I am grateful to Jerry Pattillo for his insights on this concept.

given to the faithful to rule in the world of the future.

> *Therefore also we have as our ambition, whether at home or absent, to be pleasing to Him. For we must all appear before the judgment seat of Christ, that each one may be recompensed for his deeds in the body, according to what he has done, whether good or bad. Therefore knowing the fear of the Lord, we persuade men, but we are made manifest to God; and I hope that we are made manifest also in your consciences. (2 Corinthians 5:9-10)*

> *For to this end Christ died and lived again, that He might be Lord both of the dead and of the living. But you, why do you judge your brother? Or you again, why do you regard your brother with contempt? For we shall all stand before the judgment seat of God. For it is written, "As I live, says the Lord, every knee shall bow to Me, And every tongue shall give praise to God." So then each one of us shall give account of himself to God. (Romans 14:9-12)*

This is why Jesus enters into the world of accounting as He tells his disciples to consider the cost and profit margin. He states:

> *For whoever wishes to save his life shall lose it; but whoever loses his life for My sake shall find it." "For what will a man be <u>profited</u>, if he <u>gains</u> the whole world, and forfeits his soul? Or what will a man give in exchange for his soul? "For the Son of Man is*

> *going to come in the glory of His Father with His angels; and will then recompense every man <u>according to his deeds.</u>* (Matthew 16:25-27)

To "save one's soul" is to be found worthy by King Jesus to rule with Him in His kingdom. The gift of eternal life is given. But the prize must be earned.

> *Do you not know that those who run in a race all run, but only one receives the prize? Run in such a way that you may win. And everyone who competes in the games exercises self-control in all things. They then do it to receive a perishable wreath, but we an imperishable. Therefore I run in such a way, as not without aim; I box in such a way, as not beating the air; but I buffet my body and make it my slave, lest possibly, after I have preached to others, I myself should be disqualified.* (1Corinthians 9:24-1)

> *Nevertheless what you have, hold fast until I come 'And he who overcomes, and he who keeps My deeds until the end, to him I will give authority over the nations; and he shall rule them with a rod of iron, as the vessels of the potter are broken to pieces, as I also have received authority from My Father.* (Revelation 2:25-27)

We need to understand, right now counts forever. The importance of this is captured by Merrill Unger as he states:

> *What I became as an obedient disciple of Christ is what I will always be. By obedience and sacrifice to*

Christ I am shaping a personality and a character that is eternal. If I enter this life for myself, for the things of the world, the personality that is shaped and formed by that kind of life ends at death, that kind of person is not eternal.[21]

A Hard Saying: A Conclusion

"If you want to save your life you will lose it. If you lose your life you will save it. " The context of these inscrutable but not inexplicable words of Jesus are spoken to His disciples right after the Apostle Peter vocalized two of the most conflicting statements: The first originating from and serving God; and the second originating from and serving the devil.

The conditions spoken by Jesus do not refer to the offer of a free gift; they are instead the clarion call to discipleship that will include the loss of life itself. The gift is free but the prize is earned. The consequences for the person who decides to give up demanding their way may be to lose that which is counted as living now, only to be rewarded with life which is life indeed (eternal life).

So what does this have to do with the suffering that comes into my life? Simply this: Suffering in this

---

[21] See Merrill F. Unger, *Unger's Bible Handbook*, (Chicago: Moody Press, 1971), 480.

life provides the means and the method for living a life that will be counted as worthy by the Lord Jesus. What we describe simply as, "well done good and faithful servant" is actually the highest form of praise from the King of the Universe. And it is from Him that such praise and honor can be bestowed upon us as we live a life that saves that which is truly valuable. Suffering provides us the opportunity to know this truth and live in light of it. It is not easy, nor is it pleasant. But this opportunity can result in eternal joy, for as the author of Hebrews 12:1-11 writes:

The Mandate
"Therefore, since we have so great a cloud of witnesses surrounding us, let us also lay aside every encumbrance, and the sin which so easily entangles us, and let us run with endurance the race that is set before us."

The Method
...fixing our eyes on Jesus, the author and perfecter of faith, who for the joy set before Him endured the cross, despising the shame, and has sat down at the right hand of the throne of God. For consider Him who has endured such hostility by sinners against Himself, so that you may not grow weary and lose heart. You have not yet resisted to the point of shedding blood in your striving against sin; and you have forgotten the exhortation which is addressed to you as sons, "My son, do not regard lightly the discipline of the Lord, Nor faint when

> you are reproved by Him; For those whom the Lord loves He disciplines, And He scourges every son whom He receives." It is for discipline that you endure; God deals with you as with sons; for what son is there whom his father does not discipline? But if you are without discipline, of which all have become partakers, then you are illegitimate children and not sons.
>
> ### The Model
> *Furthermore, we had earthly fathers to discipline us, and we respected them; shall we not much rather be subject to the Father of spirits, and live? For they disciplined us for a short time as seemed best to them, but He disciplines us for our good, that we may share His holiness.*
>
> ### The Motive
> *All discipline for the moment seems not to be joyful, but sorrowful; yet to those who have been trained by it, afterwards it yields the peaceful fruit of righteousness.*

This is not a promise to prevent the pain that comes to us in a variety of experiences in this life. However, it provides us with a proper purpose for our pain and suffering in this fallen and finite world in which we as Christians live out our lives. But, we must live today in light of tomorrow.

The true goal of Christian faith is more than to escape from eternal damnation, which requires one act of faith to receive the gift of eternal life (Ephesians 2:8-9; John 3:16). It is to achieve a fullness of life now and a resplendent glory in the age to come. This only happens when our faith is mature and we then obtain as our reward the "salvation of our souls." The words of Watchman Nee capture the truth:

> *The salvation of the soul demands a spirit of devotion and requires the sanity of reason; reason that delivers a man from the vanity of the world, the slavery of bodily passions, and understands we are spirit beings that came forth from God and will soon return to God. The spiritual man sees through the vanity of the world, discovers the corruption of his flesh and the blindness of his passions. Yet he is able to live by a law, which is not visible to vulgar eyes. He is able to enter into the world of the Spirit. He is able to compare and discern the greatest things, set eternity against time, and choose rather to be great in the presence of God when he dies than to have the greatest share of worldly pleasure while he lives.*

The words of Jesus as always are haunting to the spirit and halting to the mind. They should lead us to live faithfully.... No matter what!

> **"What does it profit a man to gain the whole world and forfeit his soul?"**
> Matthew 16:26

Conclusion

"Upheld by His faithfulness, assured by His forgiveness and encouraged by His promise....then the tranquility of God takes the place of our anxiety and His peace transcends our panic."
~Dave Roper~

As we come to the end let us go back to the beginning. We started our study on suffering with the creation of paradise, but we neglected to go one step before the actual creation. An infinite number of thoughts were in the mind of God from eternity past. Most of this we are not privy to; however we are made aware of a very important thought and fact that took place before the foundation of the world. In Revelation 13:8 the Apostle John writes, *"All who dwell on earth will worship him (the beast) everyone whose name has not been written before the foundation of the world* in the book of life *of the Lamb that was slain."*

What this implies and indicates is that before the creation of the world there existed what is called "the book of life of the

Lamb that was slain." Clearly we know from progressive revelation in both Old and New Testaments that it was Jesus himself who was looked upon as the suffering servant of Isaiah.

This one who was to become the crucified Christ of the Gospels is the Lamb slain before the foundation of the world. Before God had made any of the created order, He had in His mind and decreed before all time that the Lamb of God would be slain, and that the people of God would be justified by His blood; therefore being put into the book of life.

What this means is that the suffering of Jesus Christ was not an afterthought of creation but a pre-thought before any of creation. The Apostle Paul looking back into eternity said:

> *Therefore do not be ashamed of the testimony of our Lord, or of me His prisoner; but join with me in suffering for the gospel according to the power of God, who has saved us, and called us with a holy calling, not according to our works, but according to His own purpose and grace which was granted us in Christ Jesus from all eternity*
> *(2 Timothy 1:8-9)*

The grace of God was established and given to man before the creation of the ages, and from all eternity in line with the Lamb that was slain before the foundation of the world. Suffering is not an afterthought with God. It is essential; but why?

The chief end of man is to glorify God and enjoy him forever. Both Old and New Testaments continuously proclaim that in all we do we are to give glory to God. Therefore it should not surprise us that before the heavens existed, before the creation occurred within the mind of the sovereign God, it was determined that the greatest way to accomplish His greatest glory and the greatest good would be through the suffering and the slaying of the Lamb of God. The Old Testament points to the Passover. In the New Testament the Apostle John declares Jesus is the Lamb of God who takes away the sins of the world. The shadow becomes the light and the type gives way to the antitype. But this can only be accomplished through suffering on the cross, including death resulting in salvation and the glory of God.

The New Testament declares that all Jesus did was for the glory of God and was accomplished by suffering. As Saint Anselm said, *"Jesus did not come into the world out of curiosity or personal need. The Father sent Him on an errand of mercy solely to accomplish our redemption."* That redemption came at a price. And the price was the Sinless One became sin for mankind. (2 Corinthians 5:20) And so we see that suffering is the essence of the life of Jesus and the plan of God. The Apostle Paul in Galatians 3:13 states that Christ redeemed us from the curse of law by becoming a curse for us; for it is written, cursed is everyone who is hanged on a tree. The great exchange was the wrath of God that I deserved being placed upon Christ who deserved none.

The Apostle Peter reminds us that He bore our sins in His body on the tree and He was wounded for our transgressions, and crushed for our iniquities thus affirming the prophetic scriptures of Isaiah, *"by His stripes we are healed."* (I Peter 2:24; Isaiah 53:5)

The Apostle Paul in Philippians 2:8 reminds us it is by His suffering we attain the righteousness of God: *"And being found in appearance as a man, He humbled Himself by becoming obedient to the point of death, even death on a cross."*

The author of Hebrews declares:
Since then the children share in flesh and blood, He Himself likewise also partook of the same, that through death He might render powerless him who had the power of death, that is, the devil; and might deliver those who through fear of death were subject to slavery all their lives." (Hebrews 2:14-15)

The plan of God in creation was established before creation and decreed that the Lamb of God would suffer and be slain. The death of the only fully innocent person was the greatest way to bring the greatest glory to God. It should come as no surprise that God's plans have not changed; suffering now - glory later.

As to this salvation, the prophets who prophesied of the grace that would come to you made careful search and inquiry, seeking to know what person or time the Spirit of Christ within them was indicating as He predicted the sufferings of Christ and the glories to follow. (1Peter 1:10-11)

The Sovereignty of God and the suffering of humanity are not incompatible.

> *God moves in a mysterious way, His wonders to perform; He plants His footsteps in the sea, and rides upon the storm.* ~William Cowper~

Joseph also came to understand: "You (his brothers) meant it for evil but God meant it for good." (Genesis 50) The plan of God is to result in glory for God. The person of God, evidenced by His grace manifested by His provision of the Son and the power of the Holy Spirit, permit us to have all we need to live a life of godliness. The model of Jesus is manifested as scripture declares;

> *Therefore, since we have so great a cloud of witnesses surrounding us, let us also lay aside every encumbrance, and the sin which so easily entangles us, and let us run with endurance the race that is set before us, fixing our eyes on Jesus, the author and perfecter of faith, who for the joy set before Him endured the cross, despising the shame, and has sat down at the right hand of the throne of God. For consider Him who has endured such hostility by sinners against Himself, so that you may not grow weary and lose heart."* (Hebrews 12:1-3)

I cannot promise you that your suffering will stop or diminish. I cannot tell you that the circumstances you find yourself living in will change. I can tell you that you have *what* you need to live a life of victory because you have *Who* you need to endure and be victorious.

This is not easy in the midst of pain and suffering of any type. But if what the scripture says is true, then we have God's promise, provision, and power to make us able to stand until the day when faith becomes sight and we see Him. But more importantly, He sees us and says, "well done my friend, well done my good and faithful servant. Enter into the joy of your Master." The joy is nothing less than to be found worthy to be selected to rule and reign over Paradise restored, the Kingdom of God. As Jesus promised, *"And he who overcomes, and he who keeps My deeds until the end, to him I will give authority over the nations; and he shall rule them with a rod of iron, as the vessels of the potter are broken to pieces, as I also have received authority from My Father."* (Revelation 2:26-27)

It truly sounds like right now counts forever.

It is said that last words are lasting words. As we live today in light of *that day* might we hear and believe the words of F.B. Meyer:

> *It is in proportion as we see God's will in the various events of life and surrender ourselves either to bear it or do it, that we shall find earth's bitter circumstances becoming sweet and its hard things easy.*

As we invest our lives for the glory of God we must remember three theological truths that have practical implications for our lives.

- God is *sovereign* and good.
- God allows His people to *suffer* for a greater good.
- God desires that we would *serve* one another as we suffer together.

It is my sincere desire that in this book you not only find hope and help in living your life, but that you find Jesus who is our divine comforter, and companion, who suffered first so that we might be saved forever.

~Serving Him with you, until He comes for us~

Grace Line Ministry

The purpose of Grace Line Ministry is to motivate Christians toward spiritual maturity. For more information visit www.GraceLine.net

Other Publications by Dr. Chay:

- *The Faith That Saves-The Nature of Faith in the New Testament*, Wipf and Stock Publishers

- *The Glorious Grace of God- Understanding Free Grace Theology*, Grace Line Publication

- *Legalism is Lethal in the Spiritual Life*, Grace Line Publication

- *Medical Ethics*, Christian Medical Association and the Paul Tournier Institute

Grace Line is a 501 c-3 nonprofit ministry

Suffering Successfully